Trade Unions in Kenya's War of Independence
Kenya Resist No. 2

Selection from the book by Shiraz Durrani *Kenya's War of Independence' Mau Mau and its Legacy of Resistance to Colonialism and Imperialism' 1948-1990* (2018, Nairobi: Vita Books). Material on Makhan Singh from Durani, Shiraz (Ed.): *Makhan Singh; A Revolutionary Kenyan Trade Unionist.* 1915. Nairobi: Vita Books.

Kenya Resists
No.2 (2018)

VITA BOOKS

P.O Box 62501-00200

Nairobi. Kenya

http://vitabooks.co.uk

info.vitabkske@gmail.com; info@vitabooks.co.uk

Series: Kenya Resists No.2

Distributed Worldwide by:

African Books Collective

PO BOX 721

Oxford, OX1 9EN

orders@africanbookscollective.com

www.africanbookscollective.com

ISBN 978-9966-1890-9-7   (Paper)

ISBN 978-9966-114-53-2 (eBook)

Dedicated to
Makhan Singh, Fred Kubai, Bildad Kaggia,
Pio Gama Pinto
and all militant workers and trade unionists
for establishing the revolutionary trade union
tradition in Kenya

Contents

Preface to the Series, Kenya Resists

Looking Back to Fight Forward

People need to know their history in order to understand their past and present and chart out the desired outcomes for the future – in the tradition of "Looking back to fight forward". But in a class divided society where people do not have the power to keep their history alive, those who do have power manipulate, distort and hide historical facts and interpret history from their class perspective. They thus satisfy their class interests against the interest of working people.

Kenya won independence after a bloody confrontation with Britain after the sacrifices of lives, limbs, land and property of hundreds of thousands – not to mention collective punishments, unpaid, slave labour and concentration camps for millions. The sacrifices affected not only the generation involved in the war, but future generations as well. Those who fought in various ways for independence saw a minority elite, groomed under the watchful eye of imperialism, take all the power and benefits of independence.

Among the losses that working people suffered was the control over their history. Their oral histories were allowed to die with the death of those involved – directly or indirectly – in the War of Independence. Imperialism took charge of interpreting the anti colonial, anti imperialist war from their perspective, turning our heroes into villains and our enemies into heroes. Their version of history hid the achievements of people who refused to live on their knees and heaped praise on the Homeguards, the protectors of imperialist interest.

Few school textbooks depicting the reality of the war of independence exist after more than 50 years of independence; schools do not teach working class history of Kenya and radical trade unions do not feature in any curriculum – or in national consciousness. Bookshops and public libraries have poor collections on Kenyan history and even these do not show the anti-imperialist and class perspectives of the war of independence. Attempts by progressive historians and writers to address this imbalance by documenting people's perspective of Kenya's history have been ruthlessly stopped by the ruling elites directly or by intimidation. Kenya has seen over 50 years of lies, distortions, manipulation of history and hiding the loot of national wealth by the elite and their imperialist masters. And, at the same time, over 50 years of resistance to the lies, distortions, manipulation of history and hiding the loot of national wealth by working people is also hidden by the elite.

It is in this context that Vita Books has published a number of books on the progressive history of the working class and its class allies. These include titles such as *Never be Silent, Makhan Singh* and *Liberating Minds* (see further details of these books on the last pages of this Handbook or at http:vitabooks.co.uk). While the earlier books were published in London out of necessity, the situation changed with the location of the publisher to Kenya in 2016-17. The latest book – *Kenya's War of Independence* - was launched in February 2018 in Nairobi. Yet another important step by Vita Books is in addressing not only the content of its books, but to meet the needs of working people in terms of the *form* of such publications. It was felt that working people may not have time or resources to read large titles such as *Kenya's War of Independence* with its 448 pages covering over 40 years of Kenya's history.

Vita Books is therefore pleased to announce the launch of this new Series of handbooks under the title *Kenya Resists*. The new Series covers different aspects of the resistance by people of Kenya to colonialism and imperialism. The Readings are reproduced from published books, unpublished reports, research and oral or visual testimonies. Each title carries references on its particular topic to encourage readers to read and study further on these topics.

The Series aims to provide an insight into the history of resistance by people of Kenya. The Series focuses on specific aspects of resistance before and after independence, specifically Mau Mau, trade unions and peasants and nationalities. Wherever appropriate and possible, Vita Books will translate the Series into Kiswahili or relevant nationality languages so as to reach the intended audiences. In this way the Series will make historical material accessible to its intended readers.

The first titles in the Series have been taken from Shiraz Durrani's book, *Kenya's War of Independence, Mau Mau and its Legacy of Resistance to Colonialism and Imperialism, 1948-1990* (2018, Nairobi: Vita Books). Some relevant material from earlier publications is also added when appropriate. The first 3 titles to be published in the Series in 2018 are:

1. Mau Mau, the Revolutionary, Anti-Imperialist Force from Kenya 1948-63

2. Trade Unions and Kenya's War of Independence. Also includes *Reflections on the Revolutionary Legacy of Makhan Singh*. Reproduced from: Durrani, Shiraz (Ed.) 2015: Makhan Singh: a Revolutionary Kenyan Trade Unionist. Nairobi: Vita Books.

3. People's Resistance to Colonialism and Imperialism in Kenya (includes Somali, Kamba, Maasai and South Asian Kenyans, women, peasants, workers and students). It also includes presentations from the event to commemorate the revolutionary work of Shujaa Karimi Nduthu held on March 24, 2018 in Nairobi at the Professional Centre.

The choice of these three topics for the new Series is not accidental. The three aspects – Mau Mau, Trade Unions and Nationalities – make up the three pillars of resistance against the British forces. Durrani (2018) explains the significance of the three:

> Thus in essence, the War of Independence was a movement built on three pillars of resistance to colonialism and imperialism. These can be seen as Mau Mau (which included the armed and people's forces with participants from the other two pillars), the trade union movement (including all organised workers in towns and rural areas) and the people's forces consisting of peasants, national and nationality political and social organisations from across the country who supported the War of Independence in different ways, not necessarily always supporting armed resistance. (p.46).

It is necessary to see the unity of the above three forces in order to understand the process of resistance that finally forced colonialism from Kenya. A similar unity will be necessary in the struggle against imperialism and the comprador regime today.

Finally, a word about the title of the Series *Kenya Resists*. Resistance, as understood here, is resistance to colonialism, imperialism as well as to the capture of the Kenyan state by comprador forces after independence with the active connivance of imperialism. The working people of Kenya will certainly need to look back at their history in order to liberate themselves from the grip of imperialism. So we echo Bertold Brecht's call, "Reach for the book, it is a weapon" [1] –a weapon to preserve and sustain life, no less.

Shiraz Durrani
London

---

1   Available at: https://www.goodreads.com/author/quotes/26853.Bertolt_Brecht [Accessed: 16-10-17].

12-03-2018

Preface to Kenya Resists No. 2
Trade Unions and Kenya's War of Independence

It is generally known that Britain used massive force against the people of Kenya during the period when Mau Mau was active. But that force – police, civilian, military and naval – was not used only at the time of the active stage of Kenya's War of Independence. Massacres, killings, collective punishment, destruction of property and looting of land, livestock and other property were routine in the earlier period when Kenyan nationalities fought the colonial invaders.

Perhaps less well known is British violence against the trade union movement in Kenya. Just one example given below illustrates the point well.

The picture shows armoured cars parading the streets of Nairobi during the general strike of 1950, when the Kenya Government used tear gas, baton charges, Auster "spotter" aircraft, R.A.F. planes, Bren-gun carriers, armoured cars and police in order to break the strike and destroy the East African Trade Union Congress. - *Picture and caption from World Federation of Trade*

Unions (WFTU, 1952).

The question then is why did the colonial administration identify the trade union movement as a particular target of its civilian and armed attacks. Their intelligence had given a correct assessment of the danger that the organised, radical trade unions posed to the continuation of colonial and imperialist presence in Kenya. A number of factors gave strength to the trade union movement. The first was that trade unions represented the class interests of the people fighting for their rights. Colonialism – and imperialism as well – have gone to great lengths to hide the class aspect of capitalism they brought with colonialism. The trade unions, by their very existence, proclaimed that there were classes and class struggle in Kenya – before and after independence. Hence they became the target of colonialism.

Another aspect that made trade unions dangerous in the eyes of colonialism was that they were an *organised* force. Opposition to colonialism and imperialism by individuals could be managed by colonialism but it was difficult for it to manage an organised force. In addition, the trade union movement opposing the British authorities was no tame affair. It was radical and inspired by ideology and experiences from other places, particularly ideas of liberation from USSR and particularly India where colonialism had been defeated by people's forces. It was also inspired by the earlier radical movements such as the Ghadar movement which was active in Kenya, among other places.

The trade union movement in Kenya had been active ever since Britain introduced capitalist relations when it set about building the railways and imported Indian labour. Among the first strikes were as early as 1900, as documented by Singh (1969). That history points to yet other factors that Britain feared: the trade unions had no room for the divisive "tribalist" policies instigated by Britain. They were spread throughout the country, using the railways, among other means, to unite and organise the working class in the country. Plantation and other rural workers not only provided a strong link with peasants but also cemented the urban-rural split that colonialism sought to use as yet another divisive factor against the people. It was this unity that the British feared. It was a force that could not be isolated, divided and destroyed by colonialism.

Finally, the trade union movement had a committed leadership guided, not by personal greed, but a clear ideological vision in the interest of working class. Taken as a whole, these factors made the trade union movement a formidable obstacle to the colonial objectives of using the country for its own imperialist interests. And indeed, the colonial fears came true as the trade union movement understood that the *economic* interests of working class could only be safeguarded if they, at the same time, safeguarded their *political* interests. The radical trade union movement thus became active in politics and influenced the ideological direction of the progressive forces as well as in Mau Mau.

It is due to the success of the trade union movement in the national liberation movement that the colonial government suppressed prominent trade unionists like Makhan Singh, Fred Kubai, Pio Gama Pinto and Bildad Kaggia. It also passed on colonial laws to the independent Kenya government so as to ensure that future trade unions were forced to take the non-radical approach to meet worker needs. They thus created imperialist-oriented and led trade unions that bedevil working class politics to this day.

There are valuable lessons to be learnt from the history of the militant trade unions in Kenya and also from understanding how colonialism and imperialism enforced changes that made the trade unions ineffective after independence. This Series of Resistance Readings is published in the spirit of learning from our past to inform the present.

Shiraz Durrani

London
10-03-2018

Selection from: Durrani, Shiraz (2018): Kenya's War of Independence: Mau Mau and its Legacy of Resistance to Colonialism and Imperialism, 1948-1990.[2]

Trade Unions Light A Spark

Trade Unions and Mau Mau

Documenting mass dissemination of crimes of colonialism, capitalism and imperialism has become easier today with the use of social media which are bringing to light hidden facts. Dissemination of facts about the atrocities and crimes committed by the imperialism, whether in Ireland, Malaysia, Vietnam or Kenya, has become part of the daily dose of information available to the millions using Twitter and Facebook. Some examples on Twitter are Crimes of Colonialism (@crimesofcolonialism), Crimes of Britain (@crimesofbrits), Crimes of the US (@crimesofUS), Crimes of France (@crimesoffrance), Empire Exposed (@empireExposed). They bring the reality of imperialist exploitation to a generation not taught the real history that has shaped their lives. The publication of the book, Crimes of Britain: the Book in 2017 takes this information to the print medium. It is not only the crimes of colonialism that are getting wider publicity. People's resistance to colonialism and imperialism, hidden expertly by imperialism, is also now becoming part of people's consciousness. Among important media that have helped to reshape and correct people's understanding of their past, as well as the real meaning of the current exploitative workings of the military-industrial partnership led by USA, are teleSUR, Sputnik, RT, CGTN and PressTV among others. It is for this reason that many of these are under attack by imperialism. Imperialism tries to hide a real understanding of history of capitalism and people's struggles, as Petras and

---

2   Taken from pp. 82-114 of Kenya's War of Independence' Mau Mau and its Legacy of Resistance to Colonialism and Imperialism

Veltmeyer (2018) point out:

> The history of capitalism is a history of class struggle. This is because each advance in the march of capital, every assault made on working people in the quest for private profit - the driving force of capitalist development - brings about a strategic political response in the popular sector, resistance against the destructive forces engendered by this development.

An important aspect of people's resistance that imperialism seeks to hide is the role of trade unions in the fight for the liberation of workers from capitalist exploitation. What is often ignored or forgotten is the key role that the trade unions played in the War of Independence. Working class activism helped build anti-imperialist solidarity and gave an ideological framework that eventually became the economic and political demands of the War of Independence. The working class came from all parts of the country and from all nationalities and their participation in the struggles made this a national struggle. It suited colonialism and imperialism, as part of the divide and rule policy, to ignore that the working class had anything to do with the War of Independence. And it is no surprise that Kenyan comprador governments after independence, reflecting imperialist interests, have similarly ignored the role of trade unions. Trade unions were early targets of the Kenyatta government. Indeed, the concept of class is all but absent from imperialist interpretation of colonial history. This then leads to a misrepresentation of the aims and methods used by the liberation forces. But Kenya is not alone in the role of the working class being ignored and underplayed. It is the same situation for the Cuban Revolution where imperialism seeks to downplay this class resistance. As this is an important issue that affects perhaps all struggles against imperialism, it is appropriate to dwell a little on the Cuban experience as it has many similarities to the situation in Kenya. First, Quinn (2015) provides the context:

> … there remains surprisingly little documented and systematic analysis of the contribution of Cuban workers to the eventual overthrow of the detested Batista regime. Yet, as this engaging and meticulously researched book [Cushion, 2016] amply demonstrates, a militant and well-organized movement, often operating

independently of union leaders, played a pivotal role in the victory of the Cuban insurrection, not only through the final coup de grace of the 1959 general strike, but in myriad actions that served to defend workers' interests, resist state repression, and materially support the armed struggle. Thus there was a third arm to the revolutionary forces, a movement, which has been consistently ignored by general public and historians of Cuba alike.

Quinn (2015) then addresses another issue that is relevant to Kenya too. This is to do with the buying out of trade union leaders by imperialism in order to render the unions ineffective in resisting oppression. This aspect becomes particularly important in the post-independence history of Kenya when shop stewards took over leadership of union activities. Many of the strikes and other actions by workers as documented in Mwakenya's *Register of Resistance* (1986), were organised and led by shop stewards when KANU imposed leaders favourable to itself on the trade union movement. In this context, Quinn (2015) reinforces Cushion's (2016) definition of "organised labour":

> Steve Cushion's work calls for a broader definition of organized labour, looking beyond the formal structures of the trade union federation to include the multiplicity of unofficial, informal structures through which ordinary workers defend their interests. This includes the activities of shop stewards, independent minded union officials, as well as clandestine networks of militants, all of which make up the wider labour movement and interact together to produce the dynamic of industrial action.

Viewed within this expanded definition of organised labour, the record of working class in Kenya acquires a new perspective, particularly in the period before unions became better organised and led. Just as in the case of Cuba as Quinn (2015) records, in Kenya also "the final victory of the revolutionary forces should be viewed as the result of a combination of armed guerrilla action and mass support". However, the working class and Mau Mau in Kenya were overpowered by the British military presence and imperialism's use of its creation, the comprador class, programmed to prevent a revolutionary change.

And yet the part played by the organised working class was crucial in driving colonialism out of Kenya and instilling ideas of anti-imperialist struggles among people.   Drawing attention to the missing link of the contribution of organised working class was the aim of Cushion (2016) when he says:

> This book therefore challenges the notion that the revolution emerged from a rural guerrilla struggle in which the organized workers played no role and that the workers who did participate did as individual citizens rather than as part of an organized labour movement ... It is my intention to give organized labour its due credit for the role it played in the overthrow of the Batista dictatorship.

And that is the challenge to all activists and historians - "to give organised labour in Kenya the due respect for the role it played" (Cushion, 2016) in the War of Independence in Kenya. And that can be done only within the context of class analysis and class struggles before and after independence. At particular times in Kenyan history, the class aspect was not the dominant one. But the involvement of working class in that struggle was partly an aspect of their struggle against capitalism, which imposed poor and life-threatening working conditions. Release from this capitalist bondage required, first of all, national independence. It was the all-important contribution of the trade union movement, and of Makhan Singh in particular, that linked workers' economic demands with political demands as part of a working class agenda.

British colonial policy and the White Settler politics had both been focused on the need to ensure that cheap labour was regularly available for plantations, industries, settler farms and colonial government needs. This fact has again not been given the significant role it played in the political development in Kenya. While colonialism needed to take away land from peasants, they also needed labour for the capitalist venture to survive and prosper. Clayton and Savage (1974) describe these aspects graphically:

> The history of a country can be likened to a rope composed of strands of several different colours, at any one section of the rope one or two strands may appear on the surface, a third and fourth

may lie below to reappear a little distance away. In Kenya's colonial history three strands form the rope - land, labour and the action and reaction of races to one another, expressed consciously in politics. All three strands are necessary for a complete understanding of Kenyan history, but while the land and racial political strands in various periods have been the subject of close study, the study of labour has not yet received the same attention.

Thus land and labour issues in Kenya had a profound influence on Kenyan politics, not only in terms of what the Kenyan resistance forces did, but also what colonialism did and what policies they used to support their economic interests. Again, Clayton and Savage (1974) fill in the historical gaps in conventional telling of Kenyan history:

> The need to induce Africans to work, to leave their tribal societies and customs and to hire themselves to immigrant, largely British, employers also produced the very widest consequences at the local level. The size of the tribal land units, known as reserves, was the subject of early controversy, European farmers pressing for small reserves with limited funds spent on their development in order to maintain a supply of men who were obliged to work elsewhere. Taxation, instituted initially as a normal feature of administration, was used as a tool to increase labour supply. Personal identity documents were framed with labour retention and discipline as their aim. African education for many years was planned only to equip men for the semi-skilled labour market, and for a long time social services of various types existed primarily to assist the labour supply. The degree of compulsion retained by the government for the supply of its own labour needs was on occasions planned with an eye to indirect assistance to the local private employer. Trade union, minimum wage and workmen's compensation legislation were all introduced later than in other British African territories. Even relatively minor matters, the size of a proposed coinage, railway freight charges, restrictions on African dances, pass laws, and the appointment, promotion or transfer of Colonial Service officials were often influenced by the politics of the labour market.

Britain introduced capitalism and with it came classes, class divisions and, unintentionally perhaps, class struggles to Kenya. It created a vastly unequal society and then obscured the very existence of what they had created. The real beneficiaries of capitalism were well-hidden thousands of miles away in London, New York and various Western European capitals. Their local allies, initially the Settlers and later the Black elite of independence, also benefited from this imperialist venture. The Settlers were gifted land and were then able to use their unfairly acquired wealth to venture into other areas of the economy in manufacturing, import and export, banking and finance with the support of Western banking and finance. On the other side, Kenyan peasants and workers became the victims of these new class divisions, losing their land and being forced into either a serf-like situation in the countryside or as super-exploited workers tied to the Settlers as cheap labour — in the earlier period they were physically tied down with the hated kipande[3] around their necks. South Asian communities were allowed to become petty traders, civil servants and skilled workers in many industries as their skills were needed for capitalist exploitation. They became the buffers for European domination against the African population of workers, landless peasants, the newly created "squatters" and the under-employed or unemployed workers. It was this class formation that the British sought to hide from the people. They encouraged a colour, racial or tribal interpretation of what was happening in the society, as these divisions were easier to exploit than divisions by class. This enabled them to divide Kenyan people along tribal lines as part of the new social set-up, also encouraging the African peasants and workers to see the South Asians as their enemy. At the time of independence, they used this distorted interpretation of social reality to gradually incorporate the new petty-bourgeoisie into the power structure as a way of defeating the ideology of Mau Mau and undermining trade union aspirations.

The struggle of working class in Kenya has a long history and is linked with the politics of struggle for independence – and beyond. It is also linked to the input from South Asian Kenyans in terms of working class struggles from India. Gupta (1981) traces some aspects of this history and the links

---

3   Kipande: "The registration card that all African males were required to carry under
     the 1915 Registration Ordinance…the primary purpose was to enhance labour
     recruitment and control". Maxon and Ofcansky (2000).

with India:

> Ever since its origin the trade-union movement in Kenya had a sharply pronounced anti-colonial character; it developed in the struggle for national independence, for political rights and freedom. During the absence of political parties, workers' organisations were the only mass organisations representing and defending the interest of the broad masses. Struggle for the rights of the workers tended to be the struggle against the foreign capitalists who controlled the means of production.

> For many years it was difficult to separate the trade-union movement from political struggle against colonialism. During the post-second world war period, particularly during emergency (1952-61), many trade-union functionaries developed into prominent political leaders and later became high ranking statesmen of Kenya.

> Unlike many other Asian and African countries, trade unionism in Kenya originated under the influence and direct participation of Asian trade unionists, specifically Makhan Singh. The African unionists learnt union activities and assimilated the ideology and methods of the Asians. During the emergency, i.e., 1952-1961, Kenyan trade-union movement came under the influence of right-wing Socialist and Christian trade unions of Britain and the USA. The International Confederation of Free Trade Unions, through finances and advisers, gained control over the movement.

That explains the progressive period of the trade union movement before independence and its subversion by imperialism after independence.

Organising for Economic and Political Rights

There are two key strands to Kenya's War of Independence: Mau Mau and the trade union movement. The contribution of both to independence and to the struggle for rights of working class has been hidden and distorted. While the two complemented each other and fought together to undermine colonialism, imperialism has managed to give them separate identities running parallel to each other, never influencing and supporting each other. The question raised later in the book is why did Mau Mau succeed in getting independence when the earlier nationality-based resistance did not. Part of the answer is that class formation and class resistance were consolidated in the latter period. This resulted in the involvement of a militant trade union movement in the War of Independence, which then provided nation-wide perspective lacked by the nationality-based struggles of the earlier times. In addition, the trade union movement brought the perspective of class and class struggle to the forefront and this overcame the colonial-inspired divisions into "tribes" and ethnic groups.

And yet workers' and trade union activities were not confined to the rights of workers in terms of wages and conditions of employment. True, these were the essence of trade unionism, but they realised that these rights could not be achieved without active participation in the national political movement. Given the vacuum created by colonial laws which restricted nation-wide political organisations, the trade union movement filled this vacuum to give a boost to political demands of all Kenyans. In this way, workers' struggles were very closely linked to national politics and gave an impetus and guidance to national political movements. In addition, it supplied many leaders of national political organisations, who came with experience in trade unionism and awareness of classes, class contradictions and class struggles. This was greatest contribution of the trade union movement to the War of Independence and to Mau Mau. While this book does not focus on trade unions as such, it is important to see their involvement in national politics and national political organisation so as to understand better the War of Independence and the activities of Mau Mau. It should be noted that working class activism began almost as soon as capitalism created working class in Kenya, as Makhan Singh (1979) shows. Here it is important to look at some organisational aspects of organised trade union movement. The following section summarises some national political organisational work of the trade union movement. Strikes in individual industries as well as general strikes (across industries or countywide) were key tools for organising workers politically and this experience created conditions of national political activism. The following section is based on Gupta (1981) and aims to indicate the political aspects of trade unions and how it fed into the work of national political organisations and into Mau Mau.

1921

The Kenyan workers demonstrated their strength in 1921 by forming the first politico trade-union organization, the East African Association (EAA) under the leadership of a telephone operator, Harry Thuku. The East African Association (EAA) organised the resistance of plantation workers to fight against the employers' proposal, to reduce wages from 4 pence to 2.5 pence daily. There was also a government proposal to raise the Poll Tax. The Africans called their first protest meeting at Dagoretti on 24 June 1921 to protest against these proposals. This was followed by many meetings attended by thousands of Africans. In one meeting at Nairobi 20,000 workers enrolled as members of East African Association. Encouraged by this response the EAA gave a call for the first African general strike. The strike was a great success as "Thousands quit their jobs. Workers on European farms and plantations stopped work. Domestic servants refused to cook and serve food for their British employers".

1930s

In the 1930s, the trade-union movement amongst the African workers took a new turn. Under the leadership of Makhan Singh, a Marxist, an Asian worker union was set up in 1934 on East African level - the Labour Trade Union of East Africa (LTUEA). Ever since the inception of LTUEA, Makhan Singh attempted to unite African and Asian workers. This was a difficult task. Because the Asians were identified with the exploiters and were paid higher salaries. In most cases the interests of African workers clashed with those of the Asian workers. Naturally the Asian-African workers' unity could not be achieved but Makhan Singh succeeded in making the African workers conscious of trade unionism. The Asian workers' struggle influenced the African workers.

1937

Various strikes led by LTUEA took place, including one for 62 days in April. A settlement was reached with employers agreeing to a wage-increase of between 15-22%, an eight-hour week and reinstatement of all workers. [Makhan Singh,1969].

In April 1937 all Indian artisans employed in the building works demanded higher wages and to press their demand stopped all works on the new buildings in the towns. The Africans took keen interest in the struggle of the Indian workers. The Native Affairs Department Annual Report for 1937 recording this change states: "Natives have as yet no organised trade unions but there is no doubt that they took a great interest in the Indian strikes and not long after they would endeavour to form their own Union."

This struggle of the Indians helped the African political leaders realise the importance of trade unionism. So far their trade union activities were compounded with political activities. The KCA was active among workers as well. Soon they formed trade unions. Scattered workers in various industrial and service units were collected and organised under professional umbrellas. These groups became centres of class struggle, playing the historical role of economic emancipation of the working class. Initially trade unions developed out of spontaneous attempts of the workers to fight for better living conditions and higher wages. [Thus there was a] spontaneous general strike in Mombasa in 1939...

1939

Realising the importance of labour organisation, the KCA was cooperating with the Labour Trade Union of East Africa. African workers joined the Union in large numbers. In 1939 Makhan Singh celebrated May Day. This was the first time that a workers meeting was held on the workers day. The KCA President, Jesse Kariuki joined the meeting along with African workers and spoke on the occasion. Similarly three months later in July 1939 some of the KCA leaders attended the 3rd Conference of the Labour Trade Unions of East Africa. Jesse Kariuki and George K. Ndegwa, Secretary of the KCA were elected members of LTUEA.

The most significant development in Kenya trade-union movement was the August 1939 Mombasa strike. The strike began with the municipality workers for higher wages, and quickly spread to electricity, docks, post and telegraph workers in the town. Nearly 6000 African and Asian workers stopped work. The strike was sponsored by the LTUEA and supported by KCA. The LTUEA and the KCA held a solidarity meeting of Asian and African workers in Nairobi. To break the strike the government used all the high-handed methods. One hundred and fifty workers were arrested. However, the strike was a success and ended in workers' favour.

The African working class gained an invaluable experience from the Mombasa strike. It was reflected in the subsequent years' struggles. Mombasa workers provided most militant, bold and far-sighted leaders capable of leading the working class in uncompromising struggle against imperialism and exploitation of both local and foreign capitalism.

1945 - POST-SECOND WORLD WAR DEVELOPMENTS

The trade union movement in Kenya grew faster after the Second World War. The anti-imperialist movement throughout the world had gathered great momentum and working-class consciousness had greatly increased. During and after the war, there was a phenomenal rise in the urban population. Similarly there was a development of industries and other new fields of employment. The changes increased the numerical strength of the wage earning working class. On the other hand, paucity of land in the reserves pushed more and more Africans to towns.

...

The 1940s also saw the growth of nationalist movement. The ideas of democratic reforms bred by British pronouncements during the war and accession to power of the Labour Party in England helped generate political consciousness and confidence. During this period the African nationalism succeeded in over-stepping the tribal limits. The trade unions, which helped in deviating the movement from taking tribal form, gained both in strength and membership. As Barnett points out there was "a good deal of overlap in both the leadership and rank and file membership of Kenya's African political, trade union and Church school movements. Their "cross-linking" was tending to produce a single movement." The government reports also refer to the close link of trade unions and political movement. This can be seen in 1946-47 Report of the African Affairs Department of Kenya (page 49). It is stated that "For the first time Africans began to hold meetings, numbering frequently as many as 5000 people, in the Open spaces in the location (African areas)... At first these meetings were concerned chiefly with labour conditions of Africans in Nairobi but they gradually became more and more political and concerned principally with conditions outside Nairobi."

Trade-union leaders were not silent observers to Kenyan armed struggle during Mau Mau movement. The Land and Freedom Army's General China commended their work. He writes: "At that time the trade unions had the most militant leaders and were the most active groups working for independence in the city" (Itote, 1967).

1948-52

...Despite the obstacles there was a vigorous growth of trade union organisations in Kenya during 1948-52...

The rapid development of the trade-union movement made Kenyan government extremely nervous. Workers were posing threat to Settlers as well as colonial system. European Settlers charged that trade unions were being used as a weapon of political agitation and asked the government to check this tendency. Bills after bills were rushed through the Legislative Council to limit the possibilities of the growth of trade union organisations and activities. Arrests, sentences, banishment, "frame ups" and the armed force were utilised by the imperialists in a vain attempt to crush the spirit of workers of Kenya. In 1948 the hands of the Registrar of Societies were strengthened through amendment to Trade Unions and Trade Disputes Act...

The Settlers were very worried. The trade union militants were dominating national politics. Their influence on struggle for independence was increasing every day. In September 1948, Makhan Singh, the Secretary of Labour Trade Union of East Africa organised a cost of living and wages conference, the first of its kind ever held in Kenya. Delegates from more than 16 trade unions and associations participated, representing more than 10,000 African and Asian workers. The British government struck at the trade-union movement by the immediate arrest of Makhan Singh. A deportation order was made out against him despite the fact that he was a legal citizen of Kenya having been resident in Kenya since 1927 apart from a short stay in India.

In January 1949 the government and railway administration workers were banned from taking part in political activity or joining political association which, in effect seriously hampered their participation in trade-union activity and organisation. Importing of trade-union journals and periodicals from Europe and other parts of the world was also prohibited.

These restrictions had been introduced because the working class had become champions of national forces and was consistently raising the demand for loosening the fetters of British colonialism, for ending racial inequalities and privileges of the immigrant groups. The urban working class was becoming the leading factor in the development of nationalist uprising for independence. On the rural scene the landless farm workers were growing in numbers and intensifying the class contradictions. The rural and urban working classes provided the basis for the freedom movement, as they increasingly fought against colonial relationship and economic exploitation.

The increase in the number of trade-union membership pointed to a trend in political radicalism amongst the working classes. During this period trade-union leaders expressed their preference for militant nationalism. They emphasised the need for a demand for total liberation and armed struggle to achieve it. Those who supported this trend associated themselves with Mau Mau movement and the others remained at the periphery of the national struggle with commitment for independence but not for armed struggle. Kenyatta, belonged to the latter group. Bildad Kaggia, Fred Kubai, Makhan Singh, belonged to the former group.

The struggle against imperialism thus objectively became the primary aim of the Kenyan proletariat. To them imperialism was represented by the European farmers, businessmen and bureaucrats.

In Kenya the national liberation movement and working class struggle for the better conditions were interwoven and cannot be separated. Every struggle of the working class was struggle against colonial subjugation.

During the emergency in Kenya trade union movement made most rapid strides. Unfortunately, the KFL'S [Kenya Federation of Labour] financial development was financially linked with ICFTU [International Confederation of Free Trade Unions].

The above section indicates the need for bringing the resistance against colonialism right from its first steps in Kenya so as to get a better perspective of the Mau Mau period of resistance.

Classes and Class Struggle

While the British and Settler interests may have helped to hide the class divisions in the Kenya they had created, the objective facts on the ground could not be denied. Workers of all nationalities and "colours" had acted in their class interest and fought the capitalist system so as to gain their rights as workers and as an exploited class. Trade unions, ironically, got their militant outlook and organisational strength from South Asian Kenyan workers some of who were imported for their skills from colonial India to build the railways. Little did the colonialists realise that among the skills and experience that these workers would bring would include resistance to capitalism and colonialism. They came not only with their various skills needed by colonialism, but also with the ideology and experience from the struggles of the Indian working class against British and Portuguese colonialism in India. Thus capitalism created the proletariat, which, when organised as a militant force, became the source of a major challenge to colonialism, capitalism and imperialism. When this force joined hands with the militant nationalist and political forces in Kenya, the end of colonialism became inevitable. Had the armed stage not been forced upon the people of Kenya by the declaration of the Emergency, this new force would have carried on the anti-colonial, anti-capitalist struggle in Kenya perhaps with different weapons and with different results.

It is perhaps appropriate to ask why the earlier anti-colonial struggles of Kenyan nationalities did not succeed in defeating colonialism and why Mau Mau succeeded in doing so. After all, the former were fierce in their resistance, had the support of all people and had won important battles against colonialism.

What distinguishes the early resistance to colonialism from that in the 20th Century is the entry of workers and their resistance, *as a class*, against colonialism. This resistance had a number of distinguishing features that proved critical in the struggle against colonialism and imperialism. First, the organised workers saw their struggle as not only against colonialism but against capitalism and imperialism as well. This clear identification of the enemy helped them to focus on key aspects of their struggle. They also benefited from ideas and experiences of struggles from USSR and India, among others. They learnt from the earlier Ghadar struggles in Kenya and worldwide as well as participating in the Second Imperialist War. This gave them a class as well as national and an internationalist perspective.

It provided them with links with international labour movements and organisations, which again added a new dimension to the Kenyan struggle.

Another impact of the entry of working class into the War of Independence was that workers were spread all over the country and so could not be so easily isolated and defeated in one part of the country. Any attack on them became a national attack against all workers throughout the country.

In addition, the lessons of organisation and experiences in class struggles in one part of the country spread all over the country, with the railway network and railway workers carrying messages of worker resistance and strikes to workers all over the country. The aspect of trade union and Mau Mau communication systems is looked at further by Durrani, S. (2006). This gave the working class solidarity and a national perspective. It also meant that colonialism could no longer impose docile leaders on workers who had established the principle of democratic elections long before colonialism was forced to do so countrywide at a political level.

At the same time, the working class movement had strong support from peasants who had struggled over a very long time against colonialism. On its own, peasant resistance had been isolated and suppressed by colonialism. However, when the peasant militancy was added to national working class militancy, the united resistance became a mighty force that colonialism could not contain. A new dimension in the countryside is plantation and farm workers who could no longer be isolated as they got solidarity and support from trade unions.

The trade union movement and Mau Mau also benefited from the nationality-based political work of earlier generation. Harry Thuku and later KAU leaders had addressed mass meetings and formed organisations that formed the basis of later struggles. They politicised people at mass meetings and through newspapers. The establishment of independent schools movement provided a new generation of young people who were literate and were able to play an active role in different ways. Similarly, independent churches had challenged the monopoly of Christian churches, which received the blessings of colonial administration. It is therefore important not to see the War of Independence and Mau Mau and the contribution of trade unions in isolation from these earlier strands of resistance. The earlier struggles, including the massive resistance of peasants, had provided fertile ground on which the new ideas, organisations and leadership flourished.

The working class movement's contribution to the national struggle was evident in other ways too. By its very nature, it was able to transcend the artificial enmity created by colonialism between nationalities, races, gender and other divisive tactics. Workers came from all nationalities and included men and women and had national consciousness and could act nationally.

Colonialism attacked nationalities and peasants by taking away their land; workers had no land; colonialism burnt and looted peasant properties: workers had none; colonialism confiscated peasant livestock and threatened their livelihood: workers had no livestock. Colonialism's only answer to people's resistance was brute force and imprisonment of entire populations in concentration camps. While this brought much suffering to communities, it also exposed the real nature of colonialism and created a resistance mentality in people.

Just as it had no answer to people's resistance and struggle for independence in India, colonialism had no answer when trade unions in Kenya used their class weapons to challenge capitalism and colonialism and joined hands with other forces opposed to colonialism. The only weapon in the colonial arsenal, which they used against workers, was brute force. But the workers' response began to hurt their profits.

It would seem that imperialists learn no lessons from history as their solution to any of their perceived problems even today - as in Afghanistan, Iraq, Syria, Libya, Somalia - is to use their armed forces rather than seek political solutions. This approach perhaps keeps their economies going via military spending, but causes untold damage to lives of people around the world, including in imperialist countries themselves.

In the case of Kenya, the use of such military tactics *before* Mau Mau took up arms indicates that the British government had decided in advance to suppress people's demands for independence by force, as they did in Malaysia and other places. Referring to Mau Mau as terrorists was simply a way of hiding the colonial government's own military and colonial ambitions. But attacking workers in this way was counter-productive. It was like hitting themselves as, in attacking workers, they attacked their own economic interests. Their profits were based on exploiting the labour of workers and if workers stopped producing, this also stopped profits for capitalists. Thus capitalism had created a weapon that workers could use against capitalism itself. The greatest weapon that the working class brought to the colonial battlefield - potentially more powerful than the colonial armoured cars and planes — was the actual and threatened withdrawal of their labour on which capitalist exploitation was based.

But these potential advantages that the resistance movement possessed were not enough, on their own, to weaken or defeat colonialism which was strong and could not be overcome so easily. There was a need for critical ingredients, which could act as a spark to ignite a national liberation movement. And the trade unions provided this critical catalyst: working class ideology, organisation and experience from active struggles. As Singh (1969) says:

> Kenya's trade union movement has always been a part of her national struggle for resisting British imperialist colonial rule, for winning national independence, for consolidating the independence after winning it, and for bringing prosperity to the workers and peoples of Kenya.

However this truth about trade union contribution has not been accepted in many Kenyan history books. Maloba (1998) recognises the link between trade union movement and the political movement for independence:

> The political energies of Nairobi African residence was again aroused in 1949 with the formation of the East African Trade Union Congress by Makhan Singh and Fred Kubai. This union would be banned in 1950. The significance of this phase of trade unionism is that it led to a revitalization of the KAU in Nairobi, the center of widespread urban discontent. This onslaught on KAU's complacency was led by two young trade union activists, Bildad Kaggia and Fred Kubai. Both of these men were closer in temperament and radicalism to the

youth in the Nairobi slums than to the established African elite in KAU, the churches, and the administration.

Although Maloba comes closer to understanding Mau Mau than many earlier studies, he does not extend this to see the overall picture of the behind-the-scene impact of organised labour movement as an important contributory factor in the War of Independence.

It was the trade union movement that saw the links between worker struggles and national liberation as the only way of resolving the contradiction between capitalists and workers. Their awareness of the nature of their enemy is indicated in a 1936 leaflet by the Labour Trade Union of Kenya, reproduced below from Makhan Singh (1969):

> ## The struggle between capitalists and workers has started in earnest
>
> Our worker comrades! Come forward! March ahead! If you do not march ahead today, then remember that you will be crushed under the heels of capitalists tomorrow. Workers should have a united stand and should stand up strongly against the capitalists so that they should not ever have courage to attempt to exploit workers again, nor to take away workers' rights from them.
>
> Note: The workers of M/s Karsan Ladha have gone on strike for higher wages. It has been reported that the strike situation is becoming serious. This has now become a question of life or death for workers'
>
> Labour Trade Union of Kenya November 1936

But this was not the first strike in Kenya. Singh (1969) records some of the earliest strikes by workers - of all nationalities and races - in Kenya, for example:

- 1900: Railway workers strike – interestingly, this was initiated by European subordinate staff and later on "probably joined by some Indian and African workers". The strike started in

Mombasa and spread to other centres along the railway line.

- 1902: Strike by African police constables.

- 1908: Strikes of African workers at a Government farm at Mazeras and those engaged in loading railway engines.

- 1908: Strike of railway Indian workers at Kilindini harbour.

- 1908: Strike by rickshaw-pullers in Nairobi.

- 1912: Strike by African boat workers in Mombasa.

- 1912: Strike by employees of the railway goods shed in Nairobi.

- 1912: Persistent refusal to work by thousands of African workers on Settlers' farms.

There is perhaps no better record of the struggle waged by workers and their organisations than the two pioneering books by Makhan Singh (1969 and 1980). These books provide evidence of workers' militancy, which then fed into the liberation movement. It is a commentary of today's neo-colonial state of Kenya that instead of making the books part of the curricula in schools, colleges and universities, they have been allowed to go out of print.

Gachihi (1986) looks at the contribution of trade unions:

> Trade unionism among the African workers grew as a result of the appalling conditions that these workers found themselves in. The need arose to form a strong front that could represent the workers' interests effectively. In 1947 the African Workers Federation was formed under the presidency of Chege Kibachia, an African veteran trade unionist. Sporadic strikes continued right through 1947 with demands for better working conditions for African workers. These protests were flung countrywide, unlike other associations whose influence would only be strong locally. In that year, for instance, Mombasa was paralysed when the entire African labour force downed its tools in a strike.

Some highlights from the history of the labour movement may provide a better understanding of the role of the trade union movement in Kenya's liberation struggle. The Kenya Committee For Democratic Rights (1952-60) provides details of some action during the 1955 strike in Mombasa:

> · 10,000 dockworkers and others strike at Mombasa. Troops move into docks while police patrol town and docks. Troops unload military stores. Strike spread to oil companies, brewery, transport firms and aluminium companies. 4-3-55.

> · European office workers help unload liner, Kenya Castle. 5-3-55.

> · 200 Striking dockworkers stone European Mombasa Club and European cars. They also stop buses and force passengers to leave. Police reinforcements called out, two companies of the Royal Iniskilling Fusiliers leave Nairobi by train for Mombasa, and further police drafted into the port. 7-3-55.

Such strikes angered employers, the colonial government and their capitalist backers. They relentlessly attacked worker organisations and their leaders. For example, Chege Kibachia was detained for ten years for his trade union activities, as Maxon and Ofcansky (2000) relate:

> Kibachia, (1920-). Trade unionist. Born in Kiambu and educated at Alliance High School (1939-42). In 1945, Kibachia came to national attention after he moved to Mombasa to work for the East African Clothing Factory. When a general strike began in Mombasa in January 1947, the African Workers Federation was formed to articulate the demands of the strikers. Kibachia quickly emerged as its leader, first as executive officer and after March as president. As a result of Kibachia's leadership Mombasa workers won an increase in wages, and the appeal of trade unionism and industrial action spread in the colony. In August 1947, Kibachia came to Nairobi to organize a branch for the federation there, but on the 27th he was arrested. He was detained at Kabarnet for the next 10 years.

Clayton and Savage (1974) add a political connection for Chege Kibachia, that he had been "a member of KAU [Kenya African Union] and editor of the *African Leader*" and that "Kibachia told the Thacker Tribunal that he had read widely including the works of Karl Marx".

It should be noted, however, that it was not the leadership of the African Workers Federation and the leadership of the Mombasa strike alone that made Kibachia the target of colonialist attacks. The colonialists' fear was that the workers might succeed in creating a nationwide trade union organisation as Kibachia and the African Workers Federation (AWF) had opened a branch in Nairobi and planned to open branches in other towns, including Kisumu and Nakuru. In order to scupper nationwide trade unions, colonialism came down hard on Kibachia. This eventually led to the end of active life of the AWF.

Enter Makhan Singh

And that is why the entry of Makhan Singh in the trade union movement and in Kenyan politics became so important. While the overall history of the trade union movement remains outside the scope of this book, those aspects of its history that relate to its impact on the War of Independence are still relevant. And it is in these aspects that Makhan Singh played a key role. Again, the life and achievements of Makhan Singh have been dealt with in other studies, but this section looks at his work in so far as it influenced the direction of the trade union movement and in national politics.

Makhan Singh's background in trade union work and in politics helps to understand the overall stand he took. In March 1935 he was elected the Secretary of the Indian Trade Union, which was founded in 1934. He influenced it to become the Labour Trade Union of Kenya, which was open to all workers irrespective of race, religion and colour in defiance of the divisive British colonial policy at that time. Having changed the Union from Labour Trade Union of Kenya into Labour Trade Union of East Africa (LTUEA), Makhan Singh organised a successful strike of 62 days in 1937 and achieved a wage increase of between 15-25%. As a result of the successful strike, the Union's membership rose to 2,500 in Kenya and Uganda. The colonial government was forced to accept the presence of the trade union movement in Kenya. It passed the 1937 Trade Union

Ordinance under which LTUEA was registered. It is important to note that LTUEA was an overall umbrella body and the success of the strike encouraged unions to be affiliated to the LTUEA. By 1948, 16 trade unions were affiliated to LTUEA whose membership now stood at 10,000 workers. The existence of so many independent trade unions in itself is an indication of the militancy among workers.

This was a significant achievement on the part of the TU movement. Makhan Singh then had to go to India in 1939 and "within six months of his arrival [in India], he was arrested by the British government for his political activities and imprisoned for two and a half years in India. He was further restricted for two years on his release in January 1945" (Singh, 1963). During his stay in India, he studied working class conditions and the workings of the trade union movement. His work and experience in India equipped him for the coming battles in Kenya as Durrani, S. (2015b) says:

> It was during his detention [in India] that he strengthened his links with communist, socialist and other revolutionary leaders from all over India. He then worked as a sub-editor of Jang-i-Azadi [Struggle for Freedom], the weekly organ of the Punjab Committee of the Communist Party of India, until he left for Kenya in August 1947 … His exposure to new ideas, to experiences in organisational work and mass action in India had prepared him for the struggle in Kenya, both at the level of trade unionism and in the freedom struggle. The experiences with which Makhan Singh came to Kenya enriched and developed the anti-colonial and anti-imperialist struggles in Kenya.

Makhan Singh was subsequently able to influence the trade union movement in Kenya based on the experiences and ideas he acquired in India. Among these, a few are mentioned by Durrani (2015b):

> Makhan Singh saw class divisions and class struggles as the primary aspects of resistance to colonialism and to ensuring that the interests of workers, peasants and people of Kenya were in the forefront of an independent country. This was a turning point in the struggle for liberation in Kenya. Colonialism had succeeded in previous periods to divide people's struggles into "tribal" attacks on aspects of colonialism or limit them to specific locations or on specific issues,

thereby dividing forces of resistance. Makhan Singh was able to see through such divisive tactics. He had learnt lessons from his studies of Marxist literature and from his practice in India. He saw that the need in Kenya was to politicise the working class, unite them with other progressive classes and wage a struggle that would remove the causes of poverty and injustice from the country.

A particularly important contribution that Makhan Singh made, and which influenced the trade union movement as well as the War of Independence, was mentioned by Durrani, S (2015b):

> An important contribution that Makhan Singh made to the struggle for liberation in Kenya was to link the two aspects of a liberation struggle that imperialism sought to keep separate. These were economic and political aspects. Makhan Singh believed that in order to meet the economic demands of working people, it was essential to win political power first. It was only thus that foundations for an entirely different society could be laid. Makhan Singh saw the connections between economic demands of workers and the struggle for national liberation.

These and other revolutionary ideas and practices that Makhan Singh introduced into the trade union and political movements then became the mainstream of political demands of the War of Independence. Chandan (2015) mentions one such link:

> By the 1950s, new unions were forming, strikes were frequent and Makhan Singh directed trade unionism towards anti-colonial nationalist struggle, indeed the labour movement effectively turned into a militant vehicle for African political aspirations.

Newsinger (2006) also sees the radicalisation of the liberation movement as coming from the trade union movement:

> The movement [Mau Mau] was radicalised by a militant leadership that emerged from the trade union movement in Nairobi. Here the Transport and Allied Workers Union led by Fred Kubai and the Clerks and Commercial Workers Union led by Bildad Kaggia

were at the heart of the resistance. Most accounts of the Mau Mau movement either ignore or play down the role of the trade unions in the struggle, but the fact is that without their participation a sustained revolt would not have been possible.

Similarly, Kaggia (1975) examines the links between the trade union and the national political movements:

People in Nairobi looked to the trade unions for leadership, not to the 'political' leaders of KAU [Kenya African Union]. Encouraged by this support, the trade unions decided to try and capture the political leadership as well. We would begin by taking over the Nairobi branch of KAU.

For Makhan Singh, Fred Kubai and Bildad Kaggia, the political role of trade unions was essential if the needs of working people were to be met. Clayton and Savage (1974) refer this approach in connection with the latter two:

Both Fred Kubai and Bildad Kaggia regarded the E.A.T.U.C. as a ginger group to prod the K.A.U. into more dynamic political action. In practice this meant that the congress in the first four months of 1950 issued a stream of press releases and sponsored some twenty-five to thirty meetings, the tenor of which became more and more radical. It also meant that the congress supported three important strikes in 1949 and initiated a political demonstration early in 1950 which culminated a few months later in a general strike in Nairobi.

The strong links between the radical trade union movement and political organisations is what has provided strength to the War of Independence. The connection between economic and political activism, between peasant and worker struggles is highlighted by Leys (1975):

A significant group of the 'radicals' came from the trade-union movement. D. Kali and Bildad Kaggia had both worked with Kubai in the early 1950s, when a union-based group of Nairobi nationalists had tried to 'take over' KAU. Denis Akumu and O. O. Mak'anyengo were younger men, both from the historically militant and predominantly Luo dockworkers' union. Others reflected the problems of landlessness and insecurity in the countryside. This was certainly true of Kaggia, whose following was among squatters and labourers in the Rift Valley and among the landless and smaller landholders in his home area in Murang'a district, which had been a particularly bad case of malpractice in the process of land-consolidation and registration. More generally, the Kikuyu and Luo, besides being the two largest tribes in Kenya (20-7 per cent and 14-1 per cent respectively of the total African population in 1969) had experienced underdevelopment more extensively and for longer than most other tribes, though in different ways: more or less forced labour, the decimation of those conscripted for the East African military campaign, restrictions on commodity production and trade and a growing land shortage in many locations. It was natural for the nationalist movement to be largely led by Kikuyu and Luo, and equally natural for some of these leaders to arrive at a socialist position.

And so it came to be that the trade union movement entered the political arena, which then fed into the broad movement of armed resistance, Mau Mau. It was this political work of trade unions that Kenyatta's government curtailed, as Clayton and Savage (1974) record:

> The advent of the Kenyatta government led to a curtailment, but not an abolition of the trade unions. The government moved slowly, its main object being to prevent the unions from becoming a quasi-political party in opposition to the authorities. This was achieved by transforming the K.F.L. into C.O.T.U. with direct role for the Kenya President in naming the leading officials of the federation [Union]....the bargaining power of individual unions was restrained by the creation of an Industrial Court...

But that was in the future. In the period before independence militant trade unions played a crucial role in the War of Independence and that was the reason that the comprador regime came down on them so strongly. That is why the CIA invested heavily in sponsoring and training its own brand of "trade unionism" in Kenya. The CIA saw EATUC as an enemy to be eliminated. An indication of the position of the trade unions and the intensity of the on-going class and national political struggles is given by examining the content of union publicity and communications. They also indicate the aspects of classes and class struggles that the working class introduced into the War of Independence.

Another important contribution that trade unions made to the War of Independence was the establishment of links with international trade unions and other progressive organisations. These proved useful not only for developing support for Kenyan trade unions but also for Mau Mau whose struggles got a higher profile and support from such linkages. Singh (1963) mentions some of these relations:

> During 1938 the Union established relation with the British Trades Union Congress, South African Trades and Labour Council and the International Labour Office.

Such relations were in addition to those established by Makhan Singh, Pio Game Pinto and other activists with organisations in India as well as with progressive British anti-colonial organisations. Many of these organisations carried out their own research on Mau Mau and the situation in Kenya and published important publications which alerted world opinion to British oppressive behaviour in Kenya and on the struggles waged for independence by Mau Mau. Some of these publications are listed in the Bibliography and References and include S. and A. Aaronovitch, Philip Bolsover, Fenner Brockway, Frida Laski, Richard K. Pankhurst and Leonard Woolf. The publishers of such material include important political opinion-makers such as the Communist Party, the Congress of People Against Imperialism, Fabian Colonial Bureau, Kenya Committee for Democratic Rights for Kenya (London), the Union of Democratic Control and World Federation of Trade Unions. In addition, those on the mailing lists of organisations such as the Kenya Committee for Democratic Rights for Kenya (London) would have received regular newsletters, press cuttings and updates. Many activists in Kenya regularly sent reports of happenings in Kenya, particularly Pio Gama Pinto who sent regular news to his contacts in India, Mozambique and Britain; he sent these to Kenyans in Britain as well as to progressive British activists, such as Fenner Brockway. Aching Oneko, Joseph Murumbi, Mbiyu Koinange and Jomo Kenyatta were also kept well informed while in London and they passed on their news items to progressive British organisations.

The full impact of these individuals and organisations on public opinion overseas regarding Mau Mau has not been fully understood. Those who claim that Mau Mau had no external support or avenues of communications forget that there were three pillars of the War of Independence: Mau Mau, the trade unions and progressive people's force. Each made its own contribution and, taken together, provide the totality in the War of Independence.

Kenya's Trade Unions in the Context of Trade Union (TU) Struggles in Africa

Trade Unions in Kenya cannot be seen in isolation from the activities and experiences of Africa-wide trade union movement. At the same time, these activities and experiences were aspects of resistance to colonialism and imperialism. Imperialism realised the essential contribution that trade union movements were making in the people's struggles for political and economic liberation and in weakening imperialist control. While progressive trade unions and trade unionists were being banned and detained in Kenya, a similar attack on progressive trade unions in other parts of Africa was also taking place. Thus while imperialist historians failed to mention trade union contribution to the overall anti-colonial and anti-imperialist movements in Africa, imperialism was fully aware of the TU contributions. Thus they attacked not only the militant political movements but also the militant trade union movement in a silent acknowledgement of the essential unity between the two strands of people's struggles for liberation. So while on the one hand they downplayed the role of trade unions in the liberation struggle, on the other hand, they carried out covert and overt attacks on trade unions. In the case of Kenya, this involved detaining activists such as Chege Kibachia, Makhan Singh, Fred Kubai, Bildad Kaggia and Pio Gama Pinto, at the same time, banning progressive TU organisations such as the East African Trade Union Congress and African Workers Federation. The other side of the coin was to promote individuals and trade unions which opposed radical trade unions and were in more or less sympathy with the capitalist perspective on what trade unions' role should be. In the case of Kenya, this involved supporting trade unionists such as Tom Mboya and conservative trade union organisations such as the Kenya Federation of Labour.

Imperialism, however, had its own internal contradictions which saw the gradual decline of British influence on African trade unions which was then replaced by the influence of USA policies and aligned conservative trade union organisations, both national and international. Davies (1966) shows the intra-imperialist contradictions:

> Between 1953 and 1957 the Americans worked behind the scenes to erode the influence of the British in African affairs by increasing their own independent activity throughout Africa. During 1953 and 1954 the 'Mau Mau' war in Kenya provided them with an excellent opportunity.

The position of the EATUC in linking political with economic struggles was reflected on the African continent. Davies (1966) says: "Trade unionists in colonial Africa regarded the expulsion of foreign power as their primary purpose". He goes on to elaborate:

> The history of African trade unions to date is as much one of the reaction to imperial rule as to working conditions, and any study has to trace the major social changes introduced by European activity before discussing the role played in these by the unions themselves.

However, the advice from the British TUC to Kenyan trade unions was to avoid linking political with economic demands. Davis (1966) indicates the British TUC position:

> A British trade unionist was employed in Kenya as an adviser in the Labour Department, but in 1952 he was advising workers that 'a trade union is not an organization with political aims: it is an association which has as its object the regulation of relations between workers and their employers." This advice fell heavily on the ears of Kenyans whose political parties were banned and whose leaders were in detention, so that the only legal organization able to make political comments was the Kenya Federation of Labour.

However the Kenya Federation of Labour was heavily influenced by institutions and government of USA and did not support a political role for trade unions. Davies (1966) explains how the USA support for conservative voice in the trade union movement was strengthened once the progressive one was silenced by detentions and bans:

> From the Kenya labour leaders themselves the Americans possessed some distinct advantages. As representatives of the major non-communist power, they were in a position to compel respect from the British authorities. They had money ... and had an impressive network of publications and platforms which would enable the Kenya Africans to put their case before world opinion. Tom Mboya pulled out all the stops, using the international trade union press for his articles on conditions in Kenya and astutely drawing on the help of the AFL, the ICFTU, and the TUC to develop the organizational strength of the KFL and avoid a ban on its activities.

Thus was settled the role of trade unions in Kenya and Africa. Removed from political struggles of people, it soon became a mechanism to ensure the smooth functioning of a capitalist state.

Workers and Peasants Unite for Armed Resistance

It was the linking of trade union activism with the radical national political movement that provided the spark that changed the direction of the War of Independence. This led to the emergence of the armed resistance movement, Mau Mau, as the new approach to defeat colonialism and imperialism. The trade union movement provided ideological clarity and national organisational experience; the militant national political organisations provided political structures and mass support developed over a long period. The former brought the working class to the struggle, the latter brought peasants, creating a national movement of all the exploited and oppressed people. Together they formed an iron fist that colonialism fought hard to defeat. It was this combination of resistance movements that linked economic, political and social demands of the people and decided on the path of armed resistance as the way to achieve national goals.

Gachihi (1986) provides a good overview of the role that the trade union movement played in the War of Independence and in Mau Mau:

> Another facet of the prelude to Mau Mau was the growth of militant and revolutionary spirit in the trade union activities under the veteran and radical trade unionist, Makhan Singh. The role of the trade unions was significant because KAU had faced a succession of failures in its bid to effect change. Out of this failure was created the Central Committee by men who interpreted this failure to mean that much more than a reformist approach had to be adopted. Radical Africans looked to the progressive and anti-imperialist trade union movement as a viable alternative because of its national outlook and the ability to deploy workers.
>
> This spate of strikes in 1947 was felt throughout Kenya, creating in turn, radical leadership for the workers in various urban centres. One of the advantages that the Mau Mau organizers received from this was the growth of the organizational ability among men who were to become chief architects of the Mau Mau movement — men like Fred Kubai, J. M. Mungai, Bildad Kaggia and others. This radicalism in trade unions was not at first taken as an ominous sign by the Administration, but was rather regarded as a nuisance to the smooth running of state affairs. Instead of recognizing this for what it was — a militant growth of African Nationalism, — they saw, instead, the growth of 'abnormal' behaviour among the Africans. Africans were not supposed to be capable of effectively organizing themselves. Corfield, for example, did not believe that Africans could have formed or joined trade union movements or political movements as an expression of political and economic protest.

The coming together of the trade union movement and the radical politics provided the spark that was to ignite Mau Mau's War of Independence. Kinyatti (2008) provides an appropriate summary of the contribution of the trade union movement to the War of Independence:

> The EATUC leadership is credited for deepening the anti-imperialist resistance among the working class and for producing the Mau Mau revolutionary leadership. It is, therefore, important to note that the

driving forces of the Mau Mau movement were the workers, the peasants and the patriotic petty-bourgeoisie. On every level of the struggle, the working class and its proletarian leadership played the leading role.

It suits colonial and imperialist-orientated historians as well as the Kenya Establishment to bury the role of radical, organized trade unions in the liberation as they prevent the workers, the oppressed and the poor people in today's Kenya from learning of the militant past of the trade union movement and of Mau Mau.

A final point to be noted is that while organized, urban militant workers were in the forefront of the trade union movement, they had active support of rural workers, including workers in plantations and in industries generated along the railway line. Such linkages provided a nationwide perspective to the working class struggles, as did the coming together of workers from different nationalities in urban centres. Gupta 1981) makes this clear:

> The urban working class was becoming the leading factor in the development of nationalist uprising for independence. On the rural scene the landless farm workers were growing in numbers and intensifying the class contradictions. The rural and urban working classes provided the basis for the freedom movement as they increasingly fought against colonial relationship and economic exploitation.

Just as the role of peasants in the War of Independence has been side-lined by official histories, so has the contribution of rural workers not been recognised. Creating a working class and authentic history of Kenya requires all these different levels of struggles to be researched, documented and disseminated with active participation of all classes who participated in the War of Independence.

Illustrations 2: Trade Unions

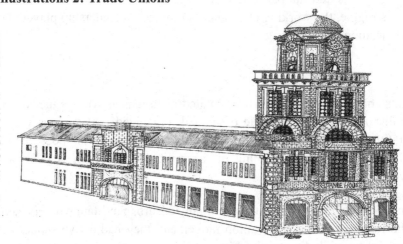

Kipande House drawn by Oswaggo, a member of the Sehemu ya Utungaji

Chege Kibachia   Bildad Kaggia

Makhan Singh

Fred Kubai

Trade Unions[4]

It was seen earlier that it was the radical trade union organisations which had injected working class ideology and leadership into the liberation struggle. As Durrani (2015a) points out:

> The working class, organised around trade union movements, played a critical role in the struggle for independence as well as in achieving the rights of working people.

Both these forces, imperialism and the neo-colonial regimes in Kenya, saw the liberation movement as a whole and the trade union movement as threats to their minority rules. Millner (1954?) explains further the reasons for attacks on the trade union movement:

> The trade union movement has been subjected to a series of attacks, over a number of years, calculated to remove all independence of thought and action and render it totally impotent.

> Trade union leaders were arrested and deported, and repressive legislation was passed, culminating in the Trade Union Ordinance, 1952, which placed the trade unions under strict control of the Government. It introduced the infamous system of "probationary" trade unions and contained elaborate provisions intended to encourage the creation of docile "employees' associations" in place of genuine trade unions.

It is clear that had a Mau Mau government come to power, it would have championed the cause of the working class and its organisation, the trade unions. This could have checked or prevented the wholesale sell-out of national wealth to comprador and corporations and prevented the continued exploitation of labour.

---

4   Taken from pp. 264 of Kenya's War of Independence' Mau Mau and its Legacy of Resistance to Colonialism and Imperialism

Three Pillars of Resistance Attacked

[5]The three pillars of resistance – Mau Mau, trade union organisations and people's forces - that were responsible for the achievement of independence were systematically attacked by imperialism and rendered powerless in order to ease the establishment of neo-colonialism. Mau Mau fighters in the forests were killed in large numbers by colonial military forces and those who continued the struggle were hunted down and killed; others who came out in good faith at independence were ruthlessly murdered by independent Kenya's armed forces.

The trade union movement was weakened by legal attacks on militant trade union movement and the banning of the EATUC and the detention of its militant leaders. But the colonial government had to use its military to supress the working class movement, just as it had done against Mau Mau guerrillas. Gupta (1981) says:

> On 28 April, the EATUC, in a 200,000 strong meeting demanded the complete independence for East African territories. Later the government refused permission to hold May Day rally. In the preceding weeks government declared the EATUC 'not a registered body', and arrested Makhan Singh and Fred Kubai on charge of being officials of an unregistered trade union." Following the arrest of Fred Kubai and Makhan Singh, within a matter of hours, the workers of Nairobi went on strike. This strike and the consequent demonstration was one of the greatest in the history of Kenyan labour movement. Unprecedented armed force was used against the workers. One would have thought a war had broken out. Not content with baton charges and tear gas, the government employed Auster spotter aircraft, RAF planes, Bren-gun carriers, armoured cars and armoured trucks. By 28 May, it was reported in the Press that at least 800 workers were behind bars.

At the same time, money from USA poured in to create a compliant trade

---

5   Taken from pp. 289 of Kenya's War of Independence' Mau Mau and its Legacy of
     Resistance to Colonialism and Imperialism

union movement under Tom Mboya. This charted a non-militant role for trade unions and strengthened the earlier colonial policy of diverting trade union movement from political struggle for independence.

The third pillar, people's forces, had been under attack by colonialism with moves such as the construction of concentration camps, detention and terror by the Homeguard and Police Reserve forces.

Thus all the avenues of militant political action were banned. The banning of opposition political parties followed. In 1969, the Kenya People's Union, the only opposition party ever to be registered in Kenya, was banned, its leadership arrested and detained. Thus ended the one chance of open politics in Kenya. All political activities now went underground as did the expression of any independent ideas and opinions. The murder of Pio Gama Pinto at his house in Nairobi in 1965 had signalled this new period of repression in Kenya. The banning of KPU completed this phase of silencing any opposition by legal or illegal means. Henceforth the battlefield shifted to the underground level.

Opposition Continues

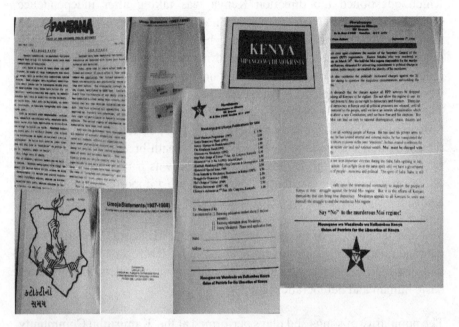

Throughout the 1970s underground groups flourished and articulated their vision of a Kenya free from capitalism and imperialism, issuing various underground pamphlets. These included *Mwanguzi* and *Kenya Twendapi* which questioned the direction Kenya was taking after independence under the new elite. Many former Mau Mau combatants began to recount their experiences and stated that they had not suffered during the anti-colonial struggles merely to see a minority elite getting all the benefits of independence. Many such views could not be published within Kenya and were published overseas. Among the best known are Karigo Muchai's The Hardcore (1973), Ngugi Kabiro's The Man in the Middle (1973) and Mohammed Mathu's The Urban Guerrilla (1974), all published in Canada by the Liberation Information Centre (LSC) with path-breaking introductions by Donald Barnett, the Director of LSC, who was part of the "collective effort" in writing and distributing one of the most important documents in Kenya's history, The Struggle for Kenya's Future. [6]

The murder in 1975 of the popular politician, J. M. Kariuki, brought out a national unanimity in anti-government feelings. It also saw the publication and distribution of a large number of underground leaflets in support of basic human and democratic rights.

The popularity of songs and plays performed at the Kamiriithu Community Centre in 1977 once again showed that the Kenyan people had rejected the elite politics and culture promoted by the government but were in support of progressive content in politics, art and drama. Events were to show that the government would not tolerate such expression of free ideas. Ngugi wa Thiong'o, one of the authors of the play performed at Kamiriithu, was detained and the open-air theatre constructed by workers and peasants was razed to ground by government bulldozers. This was the largest open-air theatre in Africa and had the added attraction that it was far from urban centres, in the countryside with peasants and local plantation and other workers forming the actors, audience and sponsors of the cultural activities. It now became clear to all that no public expression of any ideas or opinion not in agreement with imperialism was possible in Kenya. Such expression had of necessity to go underground. This lesson bore fruit in the late 1970s and 1980s when a popular underground press flourished, with a large number of leaflets being issued.

In general, the underground leaflets of 1970s reflected the contradictions

---

6   The document is reproduced in Appendix B.

of the times. Many were written by school, college and university students who played an important role in mobilising public opinion on important issues. The writers of these leaflets were also conscious, as *Africa Events* (1990a) put it, "of the class dimensions of the post-colonial Kenya society and they often tried to show the connections between Kenya's problems - not in tribal or personality lines - but in terms of what they called 'the neo-colonial path' of development opted for by the government. The leaflets bearing Kiswahili names became part of a vigorous underground press that took a very different line on national and international affairs from that of the established press."

Gradually resistance became an everyday feature of life. The extent and strength of this resistance may not immediately be obvious to a casual observer, hidden as it is by the silence of the official and corporate media. Such resistance can be examined at three levels. First, the resistance of workers, peasants, students and that of the 'whole nation'. This is the general response of the working people of Kenya to their social oppression and economic exploitation under the neo-colonial policies of the government. The second level reflects the organised, underground resistance that has given an ideological and organisational direction to the resistance of the people. The resistance at the third level was based overseas but which reflected, supported and was part of the resistance within Kenya. These two aspects of resistance - local and foreign - came together as a joint force to oppose the local ruling class and its imperialist backers.

Worker Resistance

Worker resistance throughout the country was in the forefront of direct action against oppressive laws and economic exploitation through strikes and related actions, reminiscent of the practice during the colonial period. Seen as an overall systematic resistance, these strikes and other struggles helped to build a movement against the regime, which had come down heavily against trade unions. It banned strikes and imprisoned leadership of trade unions. And, in the end, the Central Organisation of Trade Unions (COTU) was affiliated into the ruling party, KANU, thus ending its role as a workers' organisation to fight for economic and political rights of working people. But this did not suppress working class militancy as militant activists and shop stewards, isolating the official leadership, took the real leadership. Year after year, thousands of workers broke KANU laws and went on strikes for their rights.

When Moi came to power in 1978, he enforced the blind chanting of the slogan *Nyayo* demanding that people blindly follow in his footsteps without question or debate, as he was following the footsteps of the previous President, Jomo Kenyatta. A particularly significant development, indicating greater readiness to voice open opposition to the regime and to Moi personally, was the resolution passed by over 1,000 shop stewards at a meeting at Solidarity House in Nairobi to make arrangements for the Labour Day celebrations in April, 1989. They resolved that "they will answer *njaa, njaa*[7] ('hunger', 'hunger') instead of *nyayo, nyayo* to the *harambee*[8] call in the forthcoming Labour Day celebrations."[9]

The significance of this lies in the fact that the workers had bypassed the government-controlled COTU in their resistance and instead created their own organisation to continue their struggle. In addition, over a thousand activists organising and coming together was no mean an achievement in a country where a meeting of over five people was illegal if an official licence had not been obtained. Moreover the secret police monitored and suppressed any such democratic activity. The workers overcame all these obstacles to bring to the forefront the most important failure of the government - the economic mismanagement that brought vast fortunes to a select few (including Moi who was reputed to be the 5th richest man in the world) and untold misery to the majority of people.

But it is the daily struggles of the workers that gave true significance to the growing worker movement in Kenya in this period.

---

7 Njaa (Kiswahili): hunger, famine; Nyayo (Kiswahili): footsteps, referring to Moi's policy of following Kenyatta's footsteps in ensuring KANU dictatorship and pro-imperialist policies.

8 Harambee (Kiswahili): Pulling or working together. Kenyatta used the slogan to silence opposition to his rule and to extract funds from Kenyans. Most of the "voluntarily" raised funds ended up in the pockets of the elite instead of being used for the intended purpose - development projects.

9 Daily Nation, 17-04-1989.

Not willing to accept the situation, which meant daily erosion of their already very low standard of living, the workers intensified their struggles for a decent living wage and their economic, social and political rights. Mwakenya's (1987b) publication, *Kenya - Register of Resistance, 1986,* breaks down the workers' demands into three categories:

- Economic Demands: for higher wages, land and employment.

- Social Demands: safety at places of work, improved working conditions, adequate health facilities, adequate and relevant education.

- Political Demands: right to organise, right to assembly, union rights, support other workers, liberation from the entire oppressive system.

It is significant that Kenyan workers, as well as Mwakenya, saw workers' rights in the same way as Mau Mau did: that workers' rights should include social and political as well as economic rights as legitimate demands of the trade union movement. This was the key demand of the trade union movement as set up by Makhan Singh, Fred Kubai, Bildad Kaggia and others during the colonial period under the East African Trade Union Congress. This aspect is further explored in Durrani (2015b). The colonial administration, as well as the independent Kenyan government, legislated to remove workers' political rights from trade union remit - an aspect that has gravely weakened the trade union movement in Kenya. The same laws are in operation in Britain today with similar results.

Workers' resistance in this period took various forms: strikes, demonstrations, boycotts, work-to-rule, refusal to accept unfair practices. The media have been forced by the regime not to report fully on such militancy or to underplay their revolutionary significance. An examination of some worker resistance in the first few months of 1989, taken from Mwakenya (1985-89): *Upande Mwingine,* shows the extent of such resistance:

- 2000 Mombasa Municipal Council workers went on strike for more wages (January).

- 100 workers of the Gaturi Farmers Co-op Society, in Embu went on strike and demonstrated for their rightful wages (January).

- 150 workers of Nzoia County Council in Trans Nzoia went on strike for wages

- 600 workers in the open-air workshops went on strike and demonstrated when the Thika police tried to evict them from their work area. They attacked the police, many of whom were injured (January).

- 630 Kitale Municipality Workers went on strike for increased wages.

- 300 workers of the Rolmil Kenya Ltd in Kiambu went on a go-slow strike for increased wages, house allowance, leave entitlement and travelling allowance (January).

- 700 workers of the Pan-African Paper Mills, Webuye went on strike and fought police and the paramilitary GSU with stones, pieces of wood and acid (March).

- 200 workers of Lanar Road Construction Co., Bungoma held a demonstration in support for their demands for higher wages and better working conditions (April).

- 100 workers of the Athi River Mining Ltd went on strike for higher wages (May).

- 180 workers of Atta Ltd, Mombasa went on strike for higher wages in spite of being faced by armed police (May).

- 200 workers of Cosmo Plastics Ltd, Nairobi went on strike for better working conditions and right to permanent work after being considered 'casuals' after 8 years' of work (May).

- 250 workers of Afrolite Ltd, Nairobi went on strike for higher wages (June).

- 350 workers of Woodmakers (K) Ltd, Nairobi went on strike for higher wages (June).

These are just a few examples of strikes in the first six months of 1989. The actual number of workers taking strike action had been consistently increasing. Whereas 42,527 workers went on strike in 1986, the figure had jumped to 110,870 in 1988, indicating a higher level of militancy among workers. It should also be noted that as strikes were illegal in Kenya, workers going on strike risked losing their jobs and facing other "punishment". In addition, the Government's response to all strikes was to send in armed police and GSU (General Service Unit)[10] so striking workers, especially their leaders, ran the risk of being beaten up and held in remand or imprisoned where they got tortured as a matter of routine. Yet strikes continued.

Over the ten year period since Moi came to power, the situation of workers got increasingly harsh. Not only was there more unemployment (often hidden in official figures), but even those in paid employment who got the official minimum wage (not all workers got this) could not afford to maintain themselves and their families with the ever escalating price rises of basic material needs. As the International Monetary Fund (IMF) and the World Bank increased pressure for anti-worker policies, as the transnationals increased their super-profits, as Moi and those around him corruptly drained away the country's wealth, the burden of these policies fell on the shoulders of working people. The increasing number and intensity of strikes, work stoppages, demonstrations and similar actions remained the main weapons available to the working class in their struggle against a regime that sought to satisfy not the interests of the majority of people, but those of foreign and local elite who drained national resources. In this situation, there was an increase in worker militancy and strikes became routine.

Mwakenya (1987a) provides a good summary of workers' resistance

---

10 The General Service Unit (GSU) is a paramilitary wing of the Kenyan Military and Kenyan Police, consisting of highly trained police officers and special forces soldiers, transported by seven dedicated Cessnas and three Bell helicopters. Having been in existence since the late 1940s, the GSU has fought in a number of conflicts in and around Kenya, including the 1963 – 1969 Shifta War and the 1982 Kenyan coup. The Kenyan police outlines the objectives of the GSU as follows, "to deal with situations affecting internal security throughout the Republic, to be an operational force that is not intended for use on duties of a permanent static nature, and primarily, to be a reserve force to deal with special operations and civil disorders". Wikipedia. Available at: http://en.wikipedia.org/wiki/General_Service_Unit_(Kenya) [Accessed: 05-04-17].

and links it to peasants' resistance:

Workers have been hit hardest by the repressive colonial dictatorship through slave wages, arbitrary bans on strikes, police violence against striking workers and the co-option of official trade union leadership by the state. Nevertheless workers have been at the forefront in the struggle against the oppressive system. The underground workers organ Upande Mwingine shows that in 1986 alone there were over 75 cases of major strikes involving over 49,000 workers in various factories, commercial premises and other institutions all over the country. This parallels similar actions of defiant demonstrations by peasant and small traders. In the same year there were 35 recorded incidents involving over 15,000 peasants. What is documented for 1986 reflects the pattern of workers/peasants revolts since independence. Taken as a whole, the workers strikes and the peasant revolts and demonstrations between 1963 and the present amount to a mass movement against the neo-colonial economic and social system.

This naturally leads to understanding resistance by peasants.

Shiraz Durrani: Reflections on the Revolutionary Legacy of Makhan Singh [11]

Reproduced from: Durrani, Shiraz (Ed.) 2015: Makhan Singh: A Revolutionary Kenyan Trade Unionist. Nairobi: Vita Books.

A Revolutionary
Kenyan Trade Unionist

Edited by Shiraz Durrani

---

11 This is a revised version of a talk given in Nairobi on August 3rd, 2013 to mark the centenary of Makhan Singh's birth. The PowerPoint presentation of the talk was published by Vita Books in its "Notes & Quotes Study Guide" series and is available at: http://vitabooks.co.uk/wp-con- tent/uploads/sites/6/2014/08/Every-inch-a-fighter-Makhan-Singh- 03-08-13-Nairobi.pdf A shorter version of this article was published in the Communist Review No. 73 (2014), pp. 10-17.

Invitation:

December this year will mark Makhan Singh's 100th birthday. To mark this anniversary and reflect on his life and contribution to Kenya's liberation, Mau Mau Research Centre invites you to a lecture celebrating the life and work of Makhan Singh on 3rd August 2013 from 1.30pm to 4.00pm.

The highlight of the day will be a presentation by our invited speaker, Shiraz Durrani titled: "Every inch a fighter; Reflections on Makhan Singh and the trade union struggle in Kenya". The lecture will take place at the Professional Centre, St John's Gate, Parliament Road.

Highlights of the event are available at: www.youtube.com/watch?v=CByviTH5HC0&t=0s *[Accessed: 11-04-13]*

"Mr. Makhan Singh was known as "a controversial figure", "a very dangerous man", "a communist", "a born agitator" and by many other names. But to me I know him as a fighter, every inch a fighter, a Kenyan nationalist of the highest order and a brother in trade unionism and in our national struggle for independence" - Fred Kubai. Foreword to Singh, Makhan (1969): *History of Kenya's trade union movement to 1952*. Nairobi: East African Publishing House.

The "disappeared" history of Makhan Singh

The centenary of Makhan Singh's birth was on 27 December 2013. It is thus an appropriate time to assess his achievements and sacrifices so that his history can be passed on to today's youth. Since Makhan Singh's history is linked to that of Kenya and India, such an assessment will enable a correct understanding of the histories of both these countries as well as that of anti-imperialist struggles worldwide.

The entire history of anti-colonial struggles by people of Kenya has in general been suppressed or interpreted from an imperialist perspective. Similarly, struggles waged by trade unions and working class for economic and political liberation have often been seen in terms of the needs of the ruling classes. The working class, organised around trade union movements, played a critical role in the struggle for independence as well as in achieving the rights of working people. Within this struggle, Makhan Singh stands out as the towering figure who helped lay the foundation for the militant trade union movement in Kenya. It is therefore no surprise that he was the target of attacks from colonial authorities, not only in Kenya but in India as well. It is also not surprising that after independence in Kenya, the ruling class, which was no friend of the liberation movement and which stayed firmly within the US-British imperialist orbit, similarly saw Makhan

Singh as a threat to their continued control and power in post-independence Kenya.

Both these forces, imperialism and the neo-colonial regimes in Kenya, saw the liberation movement as a whole and the trade union movement at the vanguard as threats to their minority rules. In particular, they saw the liberation movement with its socialist ideology, its uncompromising leadership and its strong organisation which united working class and peasant forces as particularly dangerous for their continued survival. When the radical trade unions and progressive anti-imperialist political forces came together, they created a powerful movement that posed a major challenge to colonialism and imperialism, not only in Kenya but globally. The response from colonialism-imperialism was a military attack on the one hand, and a suppression of the three aspects of the liberation movement noted above – its ideology, its organisation and its leadership. In all these aspects, Makhan Singh was identified as one of the greatest threats, hence the harshest punishment was reserved for him.

Enter Makhan Singh

Makhan Singh played a crucial role in Kenyan people's struggle against colonialism and imperialism. His was not a narrow perspective of gaining a limited political independence under imperialism. He saw the economic as well as political liberation of working people and the achievement of a society based on principles of social justice and equality as the ultimate goals of trade union and the nationalist struggles. He saw the need for achieving the economic and political rights of working people who had been marginalised by colonialism, imperialism and ultimately by capitalism as the primary goal for people of Kenya. His vehicle for achieving his goals was the trade union movement which he did much to organise and radicalise along class lines. He realised that the economic demands of working people could be met only on the basis of becoming active on the political as well as the economic fields. He was among those Kenyans who saw clearly what the needs of the time were. He devoted his life to developing and committing himself totally to a vision of a society that was fair and just for working people. He helped set up appropriate organisational framework – in trade unions and in the political field – as a way of ensuring the achievement of his vision. He developed appropriate forms of communication to ensure people understood the working of capitalism and took necessary action at different stages of their struggle. He lived by the principles he believed in, making sacrifices which very few people were – or are - ready to make.

In spite of his revolutionary contribution to the cause of real liberation for Kenyan working people, or perhaps because of it, not many people know about him today. His achievements had been side-lined by colonialism-imperialism and also by the ruling classes in Kenya after independence. Information about his work and his enormous achievements are not in the public domain. The ideals he struggled for remain forgotten in the rush towards an unequal society created by corporate greed and sustained by the rich elite in power. Schools do not teach about him. Trade unions have been tamed into silence about him. Few are inspired by his writings, his actions and his vision for a society based on justice and fairness. As a nation, Kenya has not celebrated the crucial role that Makhan Singh played in the struggle for the rights of working people and for liberation of Kenya. And yet, his outlook, his vision and his political stand are as necessary today as they were in his time – perhaps even more so, given the globalised impoverishment of working people sponsored by capitalism in the world today. Today, we lack a visionary activist like Makhan Singh to guide us out of our current problems.

And yet there is no lack of material on and by Makhan Singh about the personal and national struggles he was involved in. He has left a vast legacy, not only of his experiences in activism and commitment to people's liberation, but also in over 20,000 documents available in the Makhan Singh Archives at the University of Nairobi. He has also left the first working class history of Kenya in the form of his two books on the history of trade unions in Kenya. Joecking (2013) confirms this marginalising of Makhan

Singh in today's Kenya when he says, "I had an A in History both in GHCR and History in form Four, but this is the first time I am hearing of Markhan [sic] Singh".

The reasons for this strange national silence about Makhan Singh are complex. But they become understandable given the geo-political situation in the capitalist world today where information has become a weapon of choice of corporations and finance capital to defend their unjust global control over wealth, power and resources. The silence is also explained by the social and political conditions in Kenya just before and after independence. Makhan Singh understood very well the social forces at play and his own position in the social and political struggles of his time. His was the voice of the working class which had been rendered powerless and condemned to poverty by forces of capitalism and imperialism. But he refused to remain silent even if this led to his detention and restriction for the longest period in the history of Kenya – this was in addition to similar treatment he suffered under the Indian colonial administration.

But colonialism-imperialism did strike a damaging blow to the twin struggles that Makhan Singh was involved in – working class and national struggles. Makhan Singh's removal from the struggle – as also of many others, including Chege Kibachia, Bildad Kaggia and Fred Kubai - made it easier for the conservative forces in Kenya, both internal and external, to marginalise working classes and divert independence into a new-colonial future. Kinyatti (2008) shows the transition from the militant stand of the radical trade unions into a "reactionary, pro-British" one:

> In 1950, the colonial state had proscribed the East African Trade Union Congress (a pro-Mau Mau, anti-imperialist trade union) and imprisoned its leadership without trial. A reactionary, pro-British element consisting of Aggrey Minya, Tom Mboya and Mucegi Karanja took over the leadership of the labour movement with the support of the British. (p.176).

Thus a lasting damage was done to the movement for workers' rights and achieving an independent nation free from imperialist manipulation. It remains a matter of speculation as to what might have happened if Makhan Singh and others had not been prevented from continuing their liberation struggles. However, it should be noted that the struggle did not die out as others took up the mantle of Makhan Singh into independence and beyond.

Classes, class divisions and class struggles

It is the existence of class divisions and class struggles that have characterised Kenya that can be seen as the reason for the silencing not only the voice of Makhan Singh but that of trade unions and working class movement as a whole. Those who saw the position that Makhan Singh took as threatening their power were the ones ensuring that his voice was silenced. That they also had political and economic power ensured that their wishes were met. Makhan Singh understood well the reality of social conflict that divided Kenyan society based on inequality and lack of social justice for working people. He described this in the following terms:

> There are two Nairobis – that of the rich and that of the poor. The status of the latter has not changed ... celebrations will be justified on the day when this country's Government becomes truly democratic, with the workers fully sharing the tasks of government (Singh, 1969, p.253).

What was true of Nairobi in 1950 was equally true at the time of independence and remains true to this day, not only for Nairobi but for the whole of Kenya. There were - and are - two Nairobis; there were – and are - two Kenyas. Kenyan society remains deeply divided into a small ruling class backed by international finance capital and the majority of working people who remain marginalised and subject to unequal laws. And it is the rich elite in power who decide which facts, which events and which personalities are to be included in "national" history. In essence, they decide whose history is to be taught, whose achievements will be part of the national narrative, and which ideas and perspectives will be "disappeared" from public consciousness. The achievements of working people, the entire Mau Mau war of liberation, the history of militant trade unionism are disappeared by the elite – together with their leaders who include Kimaathi, Bildad Kaggia, Fred Kubai and Makhan Singh. As his son, Hindpal Singh says, Makhan Singh had the "belief that the labour movement would bring prosperity and progress to the people of Kenya". It did not, and Hindpal Singh explains, "The ideology had shifted and we could not blame anybody. He was not alone [in being marginalised] because people like Kaggia, Kubai, Oneko, and Odinga suffered the same fate". (Oluoch, 2013).

This silence about Makhan Singh in the public arena in Kenya needs to be ended. The presentation made at the Nairobi meeting to mark 100 years of the birth of Makhan Singh on August 3rd, 2013 and reproduced in Appendix B is a small attempt to do just that. It provides a brief glimpse on the life and work of Makhan Singh as a way of breaking the conspiracy of silence surrounding his life and achievement. The Mau Mau Research Centre is to be congratulated for taking the initiative in organising the event.

Makhan Singh – the early years

Makhan Singh's background in Kenya and India prepared him well for the important role he was to play in both the countries. His autobiography (Singh, 1963) provides some details of his early Kenya experience:

> In June 1931, Makhan Singh began working in his father's printing press ... In March 1935 he was elected Secretary of the Indian Trade Union. In the following month he along with others induced the Indian Trade Union to change its name to Labour Trade Union of Kenya and to open its doors to all workers irrespective of race, religion, colour or creed... he remained General Secretary until August 1949 when he was elected President. (p.142).

His autobiography further relates his works in India:

> Towards the end of December 1939, he [Makhan Singh] left for

India, there to study working class conditions and the functioning of trade unionism in Bombay and Ahmedabad … in the first week of March (1940), he addressed a large mass meeting of about 30,000 Bombay workers and strikers. A few days later he attended the Ramgarh Session of the Indian National Congress as an African delegate. (p.144)

Makhan Singh was totally immersed in the freedom struggle and in the working class movement in India. For this he was arrested by the British colonial authorities on 5th May, 1940. No charges were brought against him, as his autobiography notes. It was during his detention that he strengthened his links with communist, socialist and other revolutionary leaders from all over India. He was one of the 140 detainees who went on hunger strike in 1941. He was released from detention in July 1942, but was kept under restriction within the village of Gharjakh until January 1945. In all, he was under detention and restriction in India for more than four and a half years.

He then worked as a sub-editor of *Jang-i-azadi* [*Struggle for Freedom*], the weekly organ of the Punjab Committee of the Communist Party of India, until he left for Kenya in August 1947. As his autobiography notes, "one main aim of Makhan Singh's life, the freedom of India, had been achieved". (p. 145). He next turned to his other aim – freedom and liberation in Kenya. His exposure to new ideas, to experiences in organisational work and mass action in India had prepared him for the struggle in Kenya, both at the level of trade unionism and in the freedom struggle. The experiences with which Makhan Singh came to Kenya enriched and developed the anti-colonial and anti-imperialist struggles in Kenya.

Power behind the scene

Makhan Singh took a principled stand in the struggle for the liberation of Kenya. It was this that made the colonial administration determined to take him and his ideas out of circulation by detaining and restricting him for the longest period that anyone in Kenya had suffered at the hands of colonialism. The aim was to isolate him from his base support – the working class, the trade union and the national liberation movement. Makhan Singh was a victim of the same colonial and imperialist system that today condemns hundreds of people to illegal detention in the US-run or inspired prisons in many countries of the world. The reasons for Makhan Singh's long restriction are revealed in secret Minutes of the 77th Meeting of the Council of Ministers held on 18th October 1961:

> The Governor pointed out that Makhan Singh had not at any time been tried for any offence, although he had now been in restriction for a period of 11 years. On the other hand, there was no doubt that he was a potentially dangerous person and there was evidence that he would never change his political views. (Kenya, Colony and Protectorate, 1961).

In the twisted logic of the colonial world, standing up for one's political principles was considered "dangerous" and deserving long detention – no matter that the person may have committed no offences. The above document then goes on to explain why colonialism thought that Makhan Singh was so dangerous to its rule:

> There was at present a spate of subversive societies throughout the colony and, in addition, there was within the groups which formed the Opposition in Legislative Council tense political situation brought about by the struggle between the constitutionalists and the revolutionaries. The immediate release of such person as Makhan Singh would tend to strengthen the revolutionaries... Makhan Singh had in particular a history of influence in the trade union movement and if released there was a possibility of his becoming a power behind the scenes to turn the movement in a revolutionary direction.

Thus emerges the reason for Makhan Singh's persecution. He represented the revolutionary strand of the Kenyan liberation movement whereas the colonial administration tolerated or supported the "constitutionalists", who were considered the best way for colonialism to morph into neo-colonialism and to support imperialism. From the colonial perspective, its repressive actions had helped to create a neo-colonial state in Kenya and were thus successful. The stand that Makhan Singh took would have led to real liberation for working people of Kenya, and that was considered unacceptable to the imperialist powers. That the "independent" governments of Kenya after 1963 continued the colonial-period treatment of Makhan Singh as a dangerous revolutionary is a testament to the success of the imperialist vision of the new Kenya. It is indeed ironic that Makhan Singh, who was the first one to demand and struggle for *"uhuuru sasa"*, became a victim of the *uhuru* government itself.

Makhan Singh is not alone in this imperialist-imposed isolation and marginalisation. One hears little of many other prominent activists who achieved much and sacrificed their lives in many cases for the cause of national liberation. Among them are revolutionaries like Kimaathi, Chege Kibachia, Bildad Kaggia, Fred Kubai, Pio Gama Pinto among thousands others who took up arms and resisted colonialism. In addition, there were revolutionaries throughout the period of British colonialism in Kenya who stood against the might of the colonial empire. Their histories, as that of Makhan Singh and Mau Mau, remain hidden to this day.

Early influences on Makhan Singh

Makhan Singh's autobiography (1963) mentions early influences on him which came to prominence in later years:

> During the period of his schooling in Nairobi Makhan Singh continued taking interest in world events and was influenced by the workers' and peasants' movements (both communist and socialist) and trade union struggles. At the same time he also commenced composing and reciting poems in Punjabi on religious, social and political subjects with emphasis on the struggle for freedom. (pp.141-142).

Added to this early learning, Makhan Singh continued "a serious study of political literature of all types" (Singh, 1963) when he started work at his father's printing press in 1931. He continued his learning and networking with various communist organisations in South Africa, Britain and India and studied their documents. Kenya had an early taste of anti-imperialist movements in the Ghadar movement and Makhan Singh developed his own thinking and with his own links with such organisations. Indeed many activists were hanged by British colonial authorities while many activists trained in Moscow in revolutionary theory and practice. So strong was his own influence on events in Kenya that he was targeted by imperialism as the source of major concern for them, as Kinyatti (2008) says:

> Makhan Singh was imprisoned without trial and restricted at Lokitaung until 1961. He had committed a double crime: he was a communist and a leader of the trade union movement. Since he was the key leader of the anti-imperialist labour movement, his banishment to Lokitaung, the imperialist occupiers thought, would weaken its leadership. (p.99).

A fuller, systemically conducted research into the early influences on Makhan Singh is beyond the scope of this article, yet it is urgently needed. That task is made easier with the availability of the vast resource now accessible in the Makhan Singh Archives as well as other resources on the history of Kenya – not least the recently released Colonial Files.

But what is clear is that Makhan Singh's study, learning, experiences and activities enabled him to see and act on the working-class perspectives in the on-going contradiction against colonialism and imperialism. In this he was a great educational influence on generations of activists.

Class, trade union and worker rights

Makhan Singh saw class divisions and class struggles as the primary aspects of resistance to colonialism and to ensuring that the interests of workers, peasants and people of Kenya were in the forefront of an independent country. This was a turning point in the struggle for liberation in Kenya. Colonialism had succeeded in previous periods to divide people's struggles into "tribal" attacks on aspects of colonialism or limit them to specific locations or on specific issues, thereby dividing forces of resistance. Makhan Singh was able to see through such divisive tactics. He had learnt lessons from his studies of Marxist literature and from his practice in India. He saw that the need in Kenya was to politicise the working class, unite them with other progressive classes and wage a struggle that would remove the causes of poverty and injustice from the country.

He used his experience in press work and his communication skills to present to workers and other people of Kenya an alternative perspective from that projected by colonialism and imperialism as the one to which there was no alternative. His study of the history of working class struggles in the world had shown that capitalism was not the only way to organise a society and that socialism ensured a just way of organising a society. The experience from USSR was a clear example of how an alternative system could work. For this to have an impact in Kenya, it was necessary to establish various methods of communications, including newspapers, leaflets and oral methods as well as creative means such as poetry, among others in the languages used by the people. But the crucial aspect was the content of such messages. The EATUC leaflets were clear on the class nature of the struggle in Kenya, as the following leaflets illustrate:

"The Struggle between capitalist and workers has started in earnest"

STRUGGLE BETWEEN CAPITALISTS AND WORKERS HAS STARTED IN EARNEST

Our worker comrades! Come forward! March ahead! If you do not march ahead today, then remember that you will be crushed under the heels of capitalists tomorrow. Workers should have a united stand and should stand up strongly against the capitalists so that they should not ever have the courage to attempt to exploit workers again, nor to take away workers' rights from them.

Note: The workers of M/s Karsan Ladha have gone on strike for higher wages. It has been reported that the strike situation is becoming serious. This has now become a question of life or death for workers.

- LABOUR TRADE UNION OF KENYA, November 29, 1936[88]

Makhan Singh Archives, University of Nairobi, Nairobi (translated from Gujarati by the author).

LTUEA HANDBILL, 1935 (KHALSA PRESS)

Workers' mass meeting

A workers' mass meeting will be held on Saturday, 16th January, at 5.00 p.m. in the Ramgharia Plot (Campos Ribero St.) to decide effective methods to achieve the demands of Railway artisans and the demand of 25% increase in wages from 1st April. Please do attend. Long Live Workers' Unity - Makhan Singh, Sec. Labour Trade Unions

Terms such as capitalist, workers, comrades, exploit, struggle, workers' rights - all indicate a departure from the way that Kenyan people had struggled against colonialism and imperialism in the past. Makhan Singh brought about a paradigm shift in people's thinking about their situation – and in the ways of combating this powerful enemy. So powerful was this message that imperialism had no arguments to counter such thinking. All they could do was wage a massive war against the people of Kenya and to remove the person who started this revolution in people's thinking – Makhan Singh – for over 11 years from the midst of people he led to this new way of thinking.

Achieving workers' rights

The first level that Makhan Singh fought at was to achieve workers' rights. It should be noted that resistance to Portuguese and British colonialism has been a feature of the entire colonial period in Kenya. So has the resistance of workers to the conditions they worked under. Singh (1969) records some of the earliest strike:

- 1900: railway workers strike – interestingly this was initiated by European subordinate staff and later on "probably joined by some Indian and African workers. The strike started in Mombasa and spread to other centres along the railway line.

- 1902: strike by African police constables.

- 1908: strikes of African workers at a Government farm at Mazeras and those engaged in loading railway engines

- 1908: strike of railway Indian workers at Kilindini harbour

- 1908: strike by rickshaw-pullers in Nairobi

- 1912: strike by African boat workers in Mombasa

- 1912: strike by employees of the railway goods shed in Nairobi

- 1912: persistent refusal to work by thousands of African workers on settlers' farms (pp. 6-7).

Thus there has been a long history of worker activism and formation of unions; for example, the Indian Trades Union in Mombasa and "probably in Nairobi" in 1914, the Railway Artisan Union (1922), the Trade Union Committee of Mombasa (1930), the Workers Protective Society of Kenya (1931) and the Indian Trade Union (1933) which changed its name to Kenya Indian Labour Trade Union. But unions faced a number of problems which made it difficult for them to survive. Two important impediments were mentioned by Makhan Singh (1969):

The basic difficulty was the usual one. There was no team of workers who, after having been elected officials of the union, were prepared to devote their time regularly and fearlessly to making the union function in a spirit of co-operation, unity, sacrifice and service. The reasons for the lack of such a team were not hard to find. The trade union functionaries from the very beginning had to face the general hostility of employers and the colonial rulers. The threat of victimisation by employers and/or deportation by the government was always there. (p.47).

Makhan Singh (1969) goes on to the second impediment:

There was no trade union legislation. The nature of the existing labour legislation was such that there could only be discouragement for the formation of trade unions. The migratory character of workers made the continuity of a union nearly impossible. Industry was undeveloped. There was none worth the name except the railway. That made the employment of a worker generally short-lived, so that he was compelled to go from job to job, workshop to workshop, town to town. All these factors equally affected the trade unionists. So it was no wonder that the Kenya Indian Labour Trade Union was in the same quandary as some of its predecessors. (p.47).

But this time, there was a new element in the oppressive situation: there *was* someone prepared to "to devote their time regularly and fearlessly to making the union function in a spirit of co-operation, unity, sacrifice and service." Enter Makhan Singh who became the biggest threat to employers and colonial government. So great a threat they saw in him that they detained him for over eleven years. Just one individual, with his clear vision, commitment and willingness to devote his life to the struggle and to make personal and family sacrifices was sufficient to threaten the foundation of the entire colonial-imperialist endeavour. Colonialism-imperialism found it easy to aim their bullets at armed and unarmed Mau Mau combatants and activists; they found it impossible to shoot down the ideas, the vision and the undaunted stand of Makhan Singh.

Makhan Singh's unique qualities did not go unnoticed among trade union activists of the time. Again Makhan Singh (1969) takes up the narrative:

About two months after the formation of the Kenya Indian Labour Trade Union, it became obvious that it would be difficult for the union to continue to function. In February, 1935, Makhan Singh was asked by the railway artisans if he could give a hand to help the union. He agreed. (p.49).

Makhan Singh made his presence felt in a matter of weeks. Within five weeks, the union was made non-racial. Its name was changed to the Labour Trade Union of Kenya (LTUK). "Its membership was made open to all workers irrespective of race, religion, caste, creed, colour or tribe... New officials were appointed with Gulam Mohamed (railway) as President and Makhan Singh as Honorary Secretary" (Singh, 1969, p.49).

Thus was addressed the first obstacle mentioned above. Colonialism had kept working class divided on the basis of the colour of their skin or locality, not allowing nationwide organisations. Now, Labour Trade Union of Kenya enters the scene as a nation-wide organisation, open to all workers. The result was a much strong organisation which was difficult to "divide and rule" as per colonial and employer practice. Makhan Singh (1969) recalls:

> The LTUK began to function in earnest. An office was rented... it was furnished with necessary office equipment, including a typewriter and a rotary cyclostyle machine. Meetings of the management committee and the constitution sub-committee began to take place regularly and the enrolment of members commenced. (p.50).

Thus a functioning organisation was created by Makhan Singh and it was this that changed the worker scene in Kenya. The acquirement of printing facilities enabled the trade union movement to keep workers informed about its struggles and strikes. Thus leaflets in various languages were widely circulated in Nairobi as well as throughout the areas covered by the railway line, being distributed by worker activists employed on the railways. Thus another disadvantage faced by workers – lack of communication facilities and system – which had hampered earlier actions was removed by the LTUK.

Among the early action of LTUK was to address a major worker grievance: long worker hours. Some highlights are provided by Makhan Singh (1969):

> The LTUK took up the problem of long working hours that was very prevalent at that time... on 10th August, 1935 a resolution was passed by a mass meeting of workers [which] 'condemns the action of those employers... who are weakening the workers physically and are increasing unemployment... hence it strongly demands from all the employers that in no case should they keep their employees at work for more than eight hours a day, and wages should remain as they are. (p.53).

The increasingly militant Union then set a date of October 1936 for its demands on the working hours to be accepted by employers. It is a reflection of the success of the Union's strategy and hard work that their demands were met. The Union gained the support of African workers as well and large numbers began to join the Union. "The effect of the success was felt all over Kenya and in Uganda and Tanzania too. The membership of the union went up to more than 1000", observes Makhan Singh (1969).

Following the success of this campaign, the union "decided in a mass meeting of Nairobi workers that notices be given to employers that wages of all employees be increased by 25% from 1st April, 1937" (Singh, 1969). A strike was declared to achieve this aim:

> In accordance with the plan the strike began on Thursday, the 1st April, 1937. It was a complete strike. A strike committee was formed. Picketing was organised. A free kitchen was started, where strikers and unemployed could have their food. (p.60).

The strike to support these demands lasted 62 days and ended in success: "The employers agreed in writing to a wage increase ranging from 15 to 22 per cent, an eight hour day and reinstatement of all the strikers" (p.63).

While this was a great achievement, there was another significant outcome of the strike. Singh (1963) recalls the impact of the 1937 strike for wage increase:

> The result of the victory was that Union's membership rose to about 2,500... another result was that the government came to the conclusion that the Trade Union Movement in Kenya had come to stay and that trade union legislation was necessary. A Trade Union Bill was published in the middle of May, 1937 when the strike was still continuing and it became an Ordinance in August. The Union was registered under it in September, 1937. (pp.142-143).

Thus an important requirement for any struggle, the formation of an organisation, was met.

It is of interest to note that while Makhan Singh played a crucial role in this transformation, he worked without payment. Nor does he even mention his role in the history of the period. His biography (Singh, 1963) and his two books (Singh, M. 1969 and 1980) do not mention himself in all the activities he initiated and guided, giving credit to union actions.

Thus the two obstacles mentioned earlier facing the trade union movement were removed by action by Makhan Singh. Kenya had reached a new stage in its anti-colonialism, anti-imperialism struggles.

Linking economic and political struggle

An important contribution that Makhan Singh made to the struggle for liberation in Kenya was to link the two aspects of a liberation struggle that imperialism sought to keep separate. These were economic and political aspects. Makhan Singh believed that in order to meet the economic demands of working people, it was essential to win political power first. It was only thus that foundations for an entirely different society could be laid. Makhan Singh saw the connections between economic demands of workers and the struggle for national liberation:

> Kenya's trade union movement has always been a part of her national struggle for resisting British imperialist colonial rule, for winning

national independence, for consolidating the independence after winning it, and for bringing prosperity to the workers and people of Kenya (Singh, 1969, Introduction).

Makhan Singh was the first person to make a call for independence in Kenya in 1950, but he was clear that winning independence was not an end in itself, but independence had to be consolidated to ensure prosperity for workers and people of Kenya. Ouma and Mutua (2006) explain the two aspects of Makhan Singh's work:

> The legacy of Makhan Singh points to the centrality of trade unions as one of the major epicentres of democracy. Singh wanted workers to get organised on both practical and strategic issues. The practical issues varied from housing, wages, working conditions, health, and safety among others. Strategically, he was conscious of the fact that colonialism and crude capitalism were the key foundations for the privation of workers. That is why in 1950, Singh proposed a resolution urging complete independence and sovereignty of the East African territories as the only viable solution to suffering of the people. (pp. ix-x).

Thus Makhan Singh brought together the two strands in the Kenya liberation movement – trade union and politics – which capitalism seeks to keep separate, even to this day. "He first came to prominence as secretary of the Labour Trade Union of Kenya when he organised a two-month strike in Nairobi" says Sicherman (1990, p. 178) referring to the first aspect of his work, the other being his 1950 call for independence.

A member of the Indian Communist Party, Makhan Singh "embarrassed Kenyatta and Mathu by calling for immediate independence in Kenya at a joint meeting of the Kenya African Union and the East African Indian National Congress in April 1950." Thorp, quoted in Sicherman, 1990). Seidenberg (1983, p.104) records that Makhan Singh stated that "the British Government had declared the independence of India, Burma and Ceylon; similarly it should immediately declare the independence of the

East African territories." Seidenberg (1983) further quotes Ambu Patel: "This was the first time in the history of the freedom struggle in Kenya that anyone had actually dared to make such a demand in public."

Seidenberg (1983) sums up Makhan Singh's contribution to the trade union movement in Kenya, as well as to the struggle for independence:

> With the return of Makhan Singh in August 1947, the trade union movement also acquired a radical wing. Having spent eight years in India actively participating in the trade union movement and the political struggle for independence, Makhan Singh was well-equipped to breathe new life into Kenya's labour and freedom campaign. The Labour Trade Union of East Africa formed in 1937 and later the larger East African Trade Union Congress (EATUC) formed in May 1949 became the nerve centres for activities of the more militant Asians. From 1947 until 1952, when all trade union activities were proscribed, Makhan Singh worked behind-the-scenes with prominent African trade unionists including Bildad Kaggia, Aggrey Minya and Tom Mboya. (p.97).

The colonial administration used the period before independence in 1963 to embed a system of laws that ensured that the economic struggles of working people were kept separate from their political struggles. Kubai (1969) sees the significance of the linking of these two aspects:

> I have always encountered critics who believe that our trade unions in those days were not trade unions at all in the real sense because they were politically formed and were not confined to industrial collective bargaining. This book informs them the reasons why it was necessary for the trade unions of those days to conduct their struggles not only industrially but also politically and to take an active part in the national struggle for Kenya's independence. (Kubai, 1969).

It is important to see how Makhan Singh and the trade union movement linked the economic and political struggles. The political basis of his trade union work was created by the very conditions under which capitalism operates. Ouma and Mutua (2006) see the connection:

> Singh's political work in the trade union movement was a response to the repressive colonial state generally and the labor law regime in particular. Under the colonial state – and its post-colonial successor – Kenya was imprisoned in labour laws that were designed to cheapen and exploit so-called native labor. This was the trend worldwide in the relationship between labor and capital. No wonder workers have been at the forefront of the human rights struggle over the centuries … Makhan Singh created the building blocks and pillars of the trade union movement in Kenya. (p. viii).

Such was the political and economic background that created the objective reality that Makhan Singh and the trade union movement faced. But objective factors themselves do not create change. Internal conditions have to be ready to take advantage of the objective conditions if there is going to be a major social change. Makhan Singh and others working with him helped to create appropriate organisations and trained activists to take the struggle to the next stage by putting their ideas into practice.

Makhan Singh and the progressive trade union movement he helped consolidate and radicalise recognised that for power to be attained and used effectively in the interest of working classes, some essential elements were necessary: an appropriate ideology and vision of the desired society, an organisation that could lead people to achieve its vision, and effective leadership supported by well informed and experienced activists. Without these essentials, movements and revolutions can – and are – diverted by enemies of working people, as Milne (2013) points out in the context of today's struggles:

> In the era of neoliberalism, when the ruling elite has hollowed out democracy and ensured that whoever you vote for you get the same, politically inchoate protest movements are bound to flourish. They have crucial strengths: they can change moods, ditch policies and

topple governments. But without socially rooted organisation and clear political agendas, they can flare and fizzle, or be vulnerable to hijacking or diversion by more entrenched and powerful forces.

That also goes for revolutions – and is what appears to be happening in Egypt. Many activists regard traditional political parties and movements as redundant in the internet age. But that's an argument for new forms of political and social organisation. Without it, the elites will keep control – however spectacular the protests.

And that is exactly what happened to the revolutionary trade union and liberation movement in Kenya. While the progressive forces are still to learn the full lesson of this process of marginalising popular movements by elites and imperialism, colonialism was well prepared to divert Kenyan resistance and render it ineffective by colluding with the elite it had nurtured during its entire colonial period. It was these elite that were handed over state power at independence. Kenya still has to wage – and win - the second phase of its struggle for total liberation. Lessons from earlier failures and experiences from other countries need to be urgently studied and applied today. This is also taking place in different forms in South Africa which has many parallels with the situation in Kenya in terms of this process of rendering radical movements and organisations ineffective that imperialism resorts to. It is important to hear the progressive voice from South African trade unions and activists so as to apply appropriate lessons to the situation in Kenya today, and also to understand its history correctly. What Kasrils (2013) says about South Africa can also be applied to Kenya:

> South Africa's liberation struggle reached a high point but not its zenith when we overcame apartheid rule. Back then, our hopes were high for our country given its modern industrial economy, strategic mineral resources (not only gold and diamonds), and a working class and organised trade union movement with a rich tradition of struggle. But that optimism overlooked the tenacity of the international capitalist system. From 1991 to 1996 the battle for the ANC's soul

got under way, and was eventually lost to corporate power: we were entrapped by the neoliberal economy – or, as some today cry out, we "sold our people down the river".

It was the same process of entrapment by neoliberal forces that enabled the international capitalist system to subjugate Kenya. As a result, radical leaders such as Kimaathi, Makhan Singh, Bildad Kaggia, Fred Kubai, Pio Gama Pinto, progressive organisations such as Mau Mau and the radical trade unions, and vision of a just and equal society that they aspired to were forcefully removed from the scene by a triumphant imperialism.

*

An example of how Makhan Singh linked economic and political demands of workers will indicate Makhan Singh's approach. It relates to the political demand for independence for East Africa. Seidenberg (1983) recalls the joint Indian National Congress and KAU (Kenya African Union) meeting in 1950 in response to the European Electors' Union' so-called Kenya Plan for the establishment of a British East African Dominion:

> Then Makhan Singh took the floor … he boldly moved an addendum to the resolution declaring that "complete independence and sovereignty of the East African territories" was the "real solution" and the one which should be implemented "at an early" date". In an impassioned speech, he said that the time had come for the people to unite and to demand in a single voice that the country was theirs and that no foreign power had the right to rule over it. That should be the aim of Africans, Indians and progressive Europeans. The British Government had declared the independence of India, Burma and Ceylon; similarly, it should immediately declare the independence of the East African territories. This was the first time in the history of the freedom struggle in Kenya that anyone had actually dared to make such a demand in public (p.104).

It is clear from this example that for Makhan Singh, the economic demands of working people could only be fully met once they had political power to make appropriate policies independent of corporate and finance capital interests. The real issue is which class has power to make policies, rules and regulations and in the interest of which class is the state power used. Workers' demands could only start to be met once there was political independence, hence Makhan Singh's call for independence for East Africa in 1950. This was the pre-condition for meeting the economic demands of working people.

At the same time, Makhan Singh realised that for both the struggles – economic and political – it was essential that people are politicised to understand the context of capitalism and imperialist rule which the country was under. Liberation could not come if only a few people in trade unions and politics were aware of the social and political contradictions in the society. Years of colonial education and mass media propaganda from colonialism had influenced people's thinking along a "colonial mind-set". It was thus the entire population that had to be "activated" by the provision of appropriate information and knowledge that was based on progressive, people-orientated ideas, values and experiences. Makhan Singh and the trade union movement that he led were active in various communication activities – including oral, pamphlets and newspapers.

The trade union movement influences Mau Mau

Yet another area that many have ignored or dismissed is the influence of Makhan Singh and the trade union movement on Mau Mau, the national liberation movement. As we saw earlier, Makhan Singh was active in India in trade unionism as well as in the struggle for independence from Britain. Similarly, he had these two aims in Kenya.

It is necessary to see the struggle for independence in its wider perspective. The role of the trade union movement and that of militant trade unionists such as Fred Kubai, Bildad Kaggia and Makhan Singh in the achievement of independence has generally been side-lined in the writing of the history of Kenya which has been influenced by colonial and imperialist scholarship. They brought radical working class ideology, organisation and leadership to the national liberation struggle. This changes the politics of the time in a fundamental way. This revolutionary change was influenced in no small way by Makhan Singh and the militant trade union movement he helped create. The isolation of the history of trade union movement from the history and politics of Kenya's struggle for independence suits imperialism. This isolation was a factor in the "forgetting" of the role and contribution of Makhan Singh from history.

It is not that the contribution that the militant, progressive trade union movement made to the struggle for independence is not well documented; it has been kept hidden in official records and history as taught in schools and colleges. It is thus not part of the national consciousness. A look at research and records on the contribution of the trade union movement to independence points the way to the need for further research on the topic. Newsinger (2006) explains the links, but he first sets the scene of the role played by Mau Mau:

> [Mau Mau] was without any doubt one of the most important revolutionary movements in the history of modern Africa and one of the most important revolutionary movements to confront the British Empire. (p.186).

But the question then arises as to where the movement got its revolutionary agenda. That important input came from the trade union movement which itself was deeply influenced by the ideology and actions of Makhan Singh. Newsinger (2006) shows the radicalisation of the movement as coming from the trade union movement:

> The movement [Mau Mau] was radicalised by a militant leadership that emerged from the trade union movement in Nairobi. Here the Transport and Allied Workers Union led by Fred Kubai and the Clerks and Commercial Workers Union led by Bildad Kaggia were at the

heart of the resistance. Most accounts of the Mau Mau movement either ignore or play down the role of the trade unions in the struggle, but the fact is that without their participation a sustained revolt would not have been possible. (p. 186).

Bildad Kaggia joined the Labour Trade Union of East Africa (LTUEA), the general trade union set up by Makhan Singh when the union he tried to set up, the Clerks and Commercial Workers Union could not be established. Later he became the president of the LTUEA. Kaggia (1975) looks at how the militant trade union movement entered the political arena and radicalised it:

People in Nairobi looked to the trade unions for leadership, not to the 'political' leaders of KAU [Kenya African Union]. Encouraged by this support, the trade unions decided to try and capture the political leadership as well. We would begin by taking over the Nairobi branch of KAU.

Thus those involved in the radical trade union movement, including Makhan Singh, had a profound impact in the national liberation movement. Chandan (Forthcoming) confirms this:

By the 1950s, new unions were forming, strikes were frequent and Makhan Singh directed trade unionism towards anti-colonial nationalist struggle, indeed the labour movement effectively turned into a militant vehicle for African political aspirations.

The full impact of Makhan Singh's contribution to the development of the radical left in Kenya will record his impact. Kinyatti (2008) hints at what is likely to emerge from such a fuller study:

The EATUC leadership is credited for (sic) deepening the anti-imperialist resistance among the working class and for producing the Mau Mau revolutionary leadership. It is, therefore, important to note that the driving forces of the Mau Mau movement were the workers, the peasants and the patriotic petty-bourgeoisie. On every level of the struggle, the working class and its proletarian leadership played the leading role.

It is this history from a working class perspective that will finally restore Makhan Singh and other progressive, committed and socialist leaders and activists to their rightful place in the history of Kenya and in the global anti-imperialist struggles.

Documenting resistance

Documenting the history of resistance is an important role that liberation forces have to undertake so as to ensure that their version of history and events is not forgotten or seen from an enemy perspective. That was certainly the case with Makhan Singh who realised the importance of documenting workers' struggles so as to ensure that the current and future generations were not brought up on a blinkered version of history. For this he left over 20,000 documents which are now available in the Makhan Singh Archives at the University of Nairobi. Makhan Singh also wrote the two most important books on the history of Kenya – "History of Kenya's Trade Union Movement to 1952" (1969, Nairobi: East African Publishing House) and "Kenya's Trade Unions, 1952-56 Crucial Years" (Ed. B. A. Ogot, 1980, Nairobi, Uzima Press). He was thus not only a prominent trade union organiser and a politician, but a historian who did much to preserve the working class history of Kenya. His political activism is indicated, for example, in the following extract from the Colonial Office files:

> Makhan published articles in the press, disseminated pamphlets and repeatedly addressed African audiences. He told them, *inter alia*, that His Majesty's Government was a 'foreign power who had no right to rule in Kenya', that the Kenya Government had introduced slavery, and that secret plans were being hatched to take more African land for the City of Nairobi. (Gt. Brit. Colonial Office).

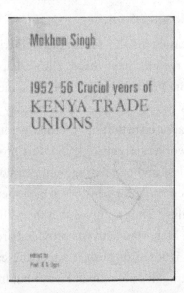

The leaflets issued during worker action provided valuable information for workers and were also a way of politicising workers to stand firm for their demands. Today they provide historical records of an important period in Kenya's history. One such leaflet is reproduced below:

5/4/1937.   126

Nairobi Workers Strike
OUR DEMANDS.

For the information of the general public and those concerned this is to notify that the demands of the workers who are on strike at various works are the following:

1   Eight hours day.
2   25 percent. increase in wages.
3   Recognisation of the Labour Trade Union of East Africa.
4   Taking back those workers who have struck.

Up till now the following employers have granted to their employers the above demands:

1   Tafail Mohamed, Contractor.
2   S. Nanak Singh, Furniture Maker.
3   Jagat Singh Bains, Contractor.
4   Karam Ali Nathoo, Box Body Maker.
5   Messrs. Thaker Singh & Co.,
6   Karam Chand, Furniture Maker.
7   N. B. Shah, Furniture Maker.

Makhan Singh,
Hon. Secretary,
Nairobi, 5.4.37.   The Labour Trade Union of E. A.

It is a measure of the success of imperialism that such documents and historical records have been allowed to remain under-used on library shelves. But this also indicates that the message and the stand that Makhan Singh took has relevance even to this day as the ruling classes still fear his message captured in the above terms - capitalist, workers, comrades, exploit, struggle, workers' rights. Again, this provides a strong indication for the working class and other struggling people in Kenya that their struggle has a legitimacy and a long history which they can draw upon for current and future battles. The examples that the militant trade unions under Makhan Singh and Mau Mau activists provided are aspects of Kenya's history that cannot be ignored or pushed under the carpet. They continue to inform people's struggles not only in Kenya but in other parts of the world as well.

It is possible today to refer to the thousands of documents left by Makhan Singh to arrive at a working class history of Kenya and also to assess the role of trade unions and of Makhan Singh himself in their challenge to imperialism. What is lacking is an appropriate academic environment which can develop scholarship around working class history of Kenya. Perhaps a Kenyan University in the future will see it fit to set up a Trade Union and Liberation Research Institute to change people's perspectives on the liberation struggle, on the role of trade unions in this and also the role of pioneers such as Makhan Singh and others currently missing from national consciousness.

Conclusion

Capitalism often has a short perspective on people's resistance to its domination over people's rights and resources. Its short-term interest is for maximum power, profits and control in the short term. Its approach is that the long-term would take care of itself - assuming the world survives the environmental degradation created by capitalism. On the other hand, those who resist imperialism, of necessity, have to have a long term perspective on their struggles, their sacrifices and their victories. Each battle lost provides lessons for the next battles; each victory strengthens the prospects for a final victory.

Thus imperialist defeat in Vietnam is easily forgotten amidst the euphoria of current victories of globalisation and new conquests, both at home and globally. Mao, Ho Chi Minh, Castro, Nkrumah, Lumumba, Kimaathi among many others are turned into villains and best forgotten. To this way of thinking, Makhan Singh is but a passing phase, easily disregarded and whose memory is sealed in dusty archives. Pio Gama Pinto matters little; Mau Mau has but little interest amidst the new conquest of the Kenyan state after independence.

Yes, people who struggle, who resist, who lose lives, land and freedom forget little. The surface may be calm. But deep waves run under the calm surface. Makhan Singh is dead, but his revolutionary legacy cannot die. It arises from the depths as a deadly tsunami to take charge of the next wage of resistance and struggle. That is the lasting – and perhaps the best – testimonial for Makhan Singh and heroes like him.

*

"People like Makhan Singh never expect any rewards. They do selfless service to whatever cause they passionately believe in, then quietly depart, leaving a great mark behind." So says Hindpal Singh (quoted in Oluoch, 2013). But this mark is such that it cannot be erased. Ever.

References

Africa Events (1990a): " Countdown to Freedom" (Cover story). Vol. 6 (8-9) August-September.

Chandan, Amarjit (2015) : Gopal Singh: An account of an EA Trade Unionist. *in* Durrani (Ed. 2015).

Clayton, Anthony and Donald C. Savage (1974): Government and Labour in Kenya, 1895-1963. London: Routledge. 2016 print.

Cushion, Steve (2016): A Hidden History of the Cuban Revolution: How the Working Class Shaped the Guerrilla Victory. New York: Monthly Review Press.

Davies, Ioan (1966): African Trade Unions. Harmondsworth: Penguin Books.

Durrani, Shiraz (2006): Never Be Silent: Publishing and Imperialism in Kenya, 1884-1963. London-Nairobi: Vita Books.

Durrani, Shiraz (Ed.) 2015: Makhan Singh: A Revolutionary Kenyan Trade Unionist. Nairobi: Vita Books.

Durrani, Shiraz (2018): Kenya's War of Independence: Mau Mau and its Legacy of Resistance to Colonialism and Imperialism, 1948-1990. Nairobi: Vita Books.

Gachihi, Margaret Wangui (1986): Role of Kikuyu Women in the Mau Mau (1986). MA Degree thesis. Nairobi: University of Nairobi.

Great Britain. Colonial Office files: "Case History of Makhan Singh". Provided by Amarjit Chandan from the National Archive Kew, England. 2014. S.C.(61)33.

Gupta, Vijay (1981): Kenya: Politics of (In)Dependence. New Delhi: People's Publishing House.

Joecking (2013): Comment in Response to Olouch (2013). Available at:

www.nation.co.ke/Features/DN2/Singh-Forgotten-hero---of-independ
ence-/-/957860/1907640/-/item/0/-/10rnmlm/-/index.html [Accessed:
31-03-14].

Kinyatti, Maina wa (2008): History of Resistance in Kenya, 1884-2002.
Nairobi: Mau Mau Research Centre.

Leys, Colin (1975): Underdevelopment in Kenya: the Political Economy of
Neo-Colonialism, 1964-1971. Nairobi: Heinemann Educational Books.

Millner, Ralph (1954?): The Right to Live. London: The Kenya Committee.

Newsinger, J. (2006): The Blood Never Dried: A People's History of the
British Empire. London: Bookmarks.

Oluoch, Fred (2013): Singh: Forgotten Hero of Independence. *Sunday
Nation*. 07-07-13. Available at: http://www.nation.co.ke/Features/
DN2/Singh-Forgotten-hero---of-independence-/-/957860/1907640/-/
item/1/-/10rnmln/-/index.html [Accessed 11-04-14].

Kasrils, Ronnie (2013): How the ANC's Faustian pact sold out South
Africa's poorest: In the early 1990s, we in the leadership of the ANC
made a serious error. Our people still paying the price. The Guardian. 24
June 2013. Available at: http://m.guardian.co.uk/commentisfree/2013/
jun/24/anc-faustian-pact-mandela-fatal-error [Accessed: 30-06-13].

Kenya, Colony and Protectorate (1961). Governor's Office. Makhan
Singh (1961). FCO 141/6870. File No. GO/POL/2/27/. Extracts from
the minutes of the 77th Meeting of the Council of Ministers held on 18th
October 1961. 1056. The Deportation (Immigrant British Subjects
Ordinance, 1949. Makhan Singh.

Kenya Committee for Democratic Rights for Kenya (London). (1952-60):
"Kenya Press Extracts". Photocopies of the Extracts available in the
Kenya Liberation Library. The Committee was based at 86 Rochester
Row, London. SW1

Kinyatti, Maina (2008): History of Resistance in Kenya, 1884-2002.

Nairobi: Mau Mau Research Centre.

Kubai, Fred (1969): Foreword to Singh, Makhan (1969): History of Kenya's Trade Union Movement to 1952. Nairobi: East African Publishing House.

Maloba, Wunyabari O. (1998): Mau Mau and Kenya: An Analysis of a Peasant Revolt. Oxford: James Currey.

Maxon, Robert & Ofcanksy, Thomas (2000) Historical Dictionary of Kenya. 2d ed. Lanham, Md & London: The Scarecrow Press.

Milne, Seumas (2013): Egypt, Brazil, Turkey: Without politics, protest is at the mercy of the elites. *The Guardian*. Available at: http://m.guardian. co.uk/commentisfree/2013/jul/02/politics-protest-elites-brazil-egypt-or ganisation?CMP=EMCNEWEML6619l2 [Accessed: 03-07-13].

Mwakenya (1987a): Draft Minimum Programme.

Mwakenya (1987b): Kenya; Register of Resistance, 1986.

Newsinger, John (2006): The Blood Never Dried: A People's History of The British Empire. London: Bookmarks.

Ogot, Bethwell A. (1980): Introduction. Singh, Makhan (1980).

Olouch, Fred (2013): Singh: Forgotten Hero of Independence. Daily Nation (Nairobi). 08-07-2013. www.nation.co.ke/Features/DN2/ Singh-Forgotten-hero---of-independence-/-/957860/1907640/-/item/0/- /10rnmlm/-/index.html. [Accessed: 08-07-13]

Ouma, Steve and Makau Mutua (2006): Foreword. Patel, Zarina (2006): Unquiet, The Life and Times of Makhan Singh. Nairobi: Zand Graphics.

Patel, Zarina (2006): Unquiet: the life and times of Makhan Singh. Nairobi: Zand graphics.

Petras, James and Henry Veltmeyer (2018): The Class Struggle in Latin America.London:Routledge.

Quinn, Kate (2015): Foreword to Cushion, S. (2016).

Sicherman, Carol. (1990): Ngugi wa Thiong'o: The Making of a Rebel: A source book in Kenyan literature and resistance. London: Hans Zell. (Documentary Research in African Literature, 1).

Singh, Makhan (1963): Comrade Makhan Singh. *in* Patel, Ambu H. (Compiler, 1963): Struggle for Release Jomo & His Colleagues. Nairobi: New Kenya Publishers. pp. 141-150. The autobiography is written in the third person.

Seidenberg, Dana April (1983): Uhuru and the Kenya Indians: The role of a minority community in Kenya politics, 1939-1963. New Delhi: Vikas.

Singh, Makhan (1963): Comrade Makhan Singh: Autobiography of the well-known Trade Unionist leader. *in*: Patel, Ambu H. (compiler, 1963): Struggle for Release Jomo and His Colleagues. Nairobi: New Kenya Publishers, pp.141-150.

Singh, Makhan (1969): History of Kenya's Trade Union Movement To 1952. Nairobi: East African Publishing House. Singh, Makhan

Singh, Makhan (1980): Kenya's Trade Unions: Crucial Years, 1952-56. Nairobi: Uzima Press.

World Federation of Trade Unions (WFTU, 1952): Terror in Kenya: The Facts Behind the Present Crisis. London: WFTU.

Every Inch A Fighter
Reflections on Makhan Singh and the Trade Union Struggle in Kenya

By

Shiraz Durrani

Presentation in Nairobi. Saturday August 3, 2013

London. UK

Every Inch A Fighter
Reflections on Makhan Singh and the Trade Union Struggle in Kenya

By
Shiraz Durrani

Nairobi. Saturday August 3, 2013

Highlights of the presentation at

http://www.youtube.com/watch?v=CByviTH5HC0&t=0s

Notes & Quotes Study Guide Series
No. 1 (2014)

ISBN 978-1-869886-02-8

http://vitabooks.co.uk

London. UK

Photo: Makhan Singh, Nairobi, 1947. Photo by Gopal Singh Chandan a quote here."

Every inch a fighter
Reflections on Makhan
Singh and the Trade Union Struggle in Kenya

Nairobi, Saturday August 3, 2013

December this year will mark Makhan Singh's 100th birthday. To mark this anniversary and reflect on his life and contribution to Kenya's liberation, Mau Mau Research Centre invites you to a lecture celebrating the life and work of Makhan Singh on 3rd August 2013 from 1.30pm to 4.00pm. The highlight of the day will be a presentation by our invited speaker, Shiraz Durrani titled: "Every inch a fighter Reflections on Makhan Singh and the trade union struggle in Kenya". The lecture will take place at the Professional Centre, St John's Gate, Parliament Road.

This Study Guide is based on the presentation made at that event. Highlights of the event can be see on YouTube at the following link:

Life and times of Makhan Singh

- Born 27-12-1913, Gharjakh, India
- 1927: Came to Kenya
- 1931: Worked in printing press
- 1939: To India
- 1940-45: Detained in India
- 1947: Returned to Kenya
- 1950-61: Imprisoned in Kenya

Makhan Singh, the trade unionist

. March, 1935: elected Secretary of the
  Indian Trade Union; Aug 1949: President
. Influenced ITU to change to Labour
  Trade Union of Kenya: open it to workers
  irrespective of race, religion, colour.
. 1937: LTUK changed to LTUEA
. April-May 1937: The Union organised
  62-day strike. Achieved wage increase
  of 15% -25% .

Patel, Ambu (1963)

Effects of strike

. The Union's membership rose to 2,500
  in Kenya and Uganda.
. The government forced to accept that
  Trade Union movement in Kenya was
  here to stay.
. 1937: Trade Union Ordinance. The
  Union was registered under it in 1937.
. By 1948, 16 TUs affiliated to LTUEA,
  with a membership of 10,000 workers.

Action in India - 1939

. Forced to go to India; studied working class conditions and TU.
. Active in India's freedom struggle.
. Addressed meeting of 30,000 Bombay workers and strikers.
. Attended the Indian National Congress as an African delegate.

1947: Back in Kenya

Sets task for South Asians

. Unite & work with Africans for democratic advancement.
. Establish democratic government with equal franchise and adult suffrage.
. Organise joint fronts of Indian Assosiations, African political unions, Pakistani organisations, Trade Unions of all workers and Youth Leagues.
. Establish common high schools. Learn Kiswahili. Teach the best of your culture, learn the best from African culture

Daily Chronicle: 12-02-1949

1947-50: independence call

. Organiser of the Kenya Youth Conference; elected Vice-President.
. Took part in E.A. Indian National Congress; a leading campaigner for 1948 local elections.
. 1949: Organised EA TUC. President: Fred Kubai; Secretary General.: Makhan Singh.
. 23-04-1950: Makhan Singh first person to call for complete independence for East Africa at mass meeting of Kenya African Union & East Africa Indian National Congress.

May Day 1950 arrest

. May Day speech: "Workers and the peoples of EA should further strengthen their unity, become more resolute and speed up the movement for freedom of all workers and peoples of E. A."
. 15th May: Makhan Singh and Fred Kubai arrested. Leads to 10 day strike.
. Demands: release arrested leaders, complete independence for EA, increase wages from 40/- to Shs.100/- p.m.

Restriction 1950-61

. Allegations against him were in connection with his Trade Union activities as Gen. Sec. of EATUC, expression of political views in the course of national struggle for freedom and being a communist.

. 5th June, 1950: Restriction Order.

. Restricted for over 11 years. During restriction, pressure was brought upon him to leave Kenya or to change his attitude: Makhan Singh did neither.

Colonial Accusation

"Makhan Singh published articles in the press, disseminated pamphlets and repeatedly addressed African audiences. He told them the HM Govt. was 'a foreign power who had no right to rule in Kenya, that Kenya Govt. had introduced slavery, that secret plans were being hatched to take more African land'.

- Throup quoted in Sicherman (1990)

1950 - 1962

- 1950s: Change forced by Mau Mau.
- 22-10-61: Makhan Singh released unconditionally.
- Nov. 1961: resumed political & TU activities.
- Resumed membership of the Printing and Kindred Trade Workers' Union (he was one of the founders).
- 1962: Elected Chair of Legislative Committee of Kenya Federation of Labour; a KFL rep. on Tripartite Committee, which drafted Industrial Relations.
- 21st October 1962: Joined KANU, when its doors of membership opened to all.

TU and national struggle linked

"Kenya's trade union movement has always been a part of her national struggle for resisting British imperialist colonial rule, for winning national independence, for consolidating the independence after winning it, and for bringing prosperity to the workers and peoples of Kenya"

- Singh, Makhan (1969)

Makhan Singh highlights the class issue

"There are two Nairobis – that of the rich and that of the poor. The status of the latter has not changed ... celebrations [to make status of City for Nairobi] will be justified on the day when this country's Government becomes truly democratic, with the workers fully sharing the tasks of government".

Our worker comrades! Come forward! March ahead! If you do not march ahead today, then remember that you will be crushed under the heels of capitalists tomorrow. Workers should have a united stand and should stand up strongly against the capitalists so that they should not ever have the courage to attempt to exploit workers again, nor to take away workers' rights from them.

Note: The workers of M/s Karsan Ladha have gone on strike for higher wages. It has been reported that the strike situation is becoming serious. This has now become a question of life or death for workers.

- LabourTrade Union of Kenya leaflet. November 29, 1936

Source: Makhan Singh Archives, Nairobi. Translated from Gujarati by the author.

LTUEA handbill, 1935 (Khalsa Press)

Workers' Mass Meeting

A workers' mass meeting will be held on Saturday, 16th January, at 5.00 p.m. in the Ramgharia Plot (Campos Ribero Street) to decide effective methods to achieve the demands of Railway artisans and the demand of 25 percent increase in wages from 1st April. Please do attend.

Long Live Workers' Unity

- Makhan Singh, Sec. Labour Trade Unions

Heroic resistance of our people

. "The heroic resistance of our people of the onslaughts of the imperialists has ultimately defeated one of the biggest imperialist powers in the world and has won our complete independence".

. "In course of my restriction for 11.5 years (May 1950 to October 1961) I continued my resistance all the time. In course of this struggle, I went on three hunger strikes.

.Lokitaung: Jan-Feb, 1952 for 10 days

.Maralal: October 1959, for 12 days

.Maralal: Started on 13-03-1961 and ended in Dol Dol on 03-04-1961 after 21 days."

- Singh, Makhan (1963)

Working class struggle, 1937

Another part of the workers' procession in 1937

Reflections on Makhan Singh's achievements and legacy

The battle of ideas

. Why is Makhan Singh not more widely known?
. Imperialism uses: distortion of history, misinformation, "disappearing" of progressive ideas, actions and people.
. Makhan Singh recorded working class history.
. He saw that communication was crucial.
. He believed a vision of an equal and just society was as essential as action to achieve it.
. Makhan Singh's example was too dangerous for imperialism, hence he, his vision and his actions have been suppressed.

Classes and class struggles

. Imperialism opposed class consciousness, class analysis and class struggles; it wanted to break working class unity and divide people by "tribes", religion, colour and race. It wanted:
. resistance to be disorganised, leaderless and without an ideology and divided.
. trade unions to focus on economic, not political, struggles.
. to create strife among working people, discord among political & trade union activists.
. Makhan Singh fought all these in ideas and action. This brought the wrath of imperialism on him.

Linking economic & political struggles

. "[Some] believe that trade unions in those days were not trade unions at all because they were politically formed and not confined to industrial collective bargaining.

. In this book, MS [explains] why it was necessary for trade unions to conduct their struggles not only industrially but also politically and to take an active part in the national struggle for Kenya's independence".

Kubai (1969)

Relations between labour and capital

. Singh's political work in the trade union movement was a response to the repressive colonial state generally and the labor law regime in particular.

. Under the colonial state – and its post-colonial successor – Kenya was imprisoned in labour laws that were designed to cheapen and exploit "native labor". This was the trend worldwide in the relationship between labor and capital.

. Workers have been at the forefront of the human rights struggle over the centuries ... Makhan Singh created the building blocks & pillars of trade union movement in Kenya.

- Ouma and Mutua (2006)

Makhan Singh's legacy

. The legacy of Makhan Singh points to the centrality of Trade Union as one of the major epicentres of democracy.
. Singh wanted workers to get organised on both practical and strategic issues. The practical issues varied from housing, wages, working conditions, health, and safety.
. Strategically, he was conscious that colonialism and crude capitalism were the key foundations for the privation of workers.
. That is why in 1950, Singh proposed a resolution urging complete independence and sovereignty of EA as the only viable solution to suffering of the people.

- Ouma and Mutua (2006)

A real revolutionary

Mwakenya celebrates Kenyan heroes in its Draft Minimum Programme, 1987

"I turned next to the trade unions after hearing Makhan Singh address the EATUC. But only Makhan agreed with my ideas. He had the fire I admired and was a real revolutionary … our Union became part of Makhan Singh's LTUEA. Later I became the president of LTUEA"
– Bildad Kaggia

Trade unions and Mau Mau

. Mau Mau was "one of the most important revolutionary movements in the history of modern Africa and one of the most important revolutionary movement to confront British Empire".

. "The movement was radicalised by a militant leadership that emerged from the trade union movement in Nairobi".

-Newsinger, John (2006)

TU provided radical leadership

. Most accounts of Mau Mau ignore or play down the role of TUs in struggle.
. Without their participation a sustained revolt would not have been possible.
. 1950: Makhan Singh, and Fred Kubai arrested; EATUC banned.
. Militants of TU threw themselves into the revolutionary movement and established themselves as a new radical leadership committed to overthrowing colonial rule by mass action, strikes, demonstrations and armed struggle".

-Newsinger, John (2006)

Parallel paths: South Africa and Kenya

. "Back then, our hopes were high for our country: modern industrial economy, strategic mineral resources, a working class and organised TU movement with a rich tradition of struggle.

. But that optimism overlooked the tenacity of the international capitalist system. From 1991 to 1996 the battle for the ANC's soul was eventually lost to corporate power: we were entrapped by the neoliberal economy – we "sold our people down the river".

- Ronnie Kasrils, 2013

Makhan Singh, the historian

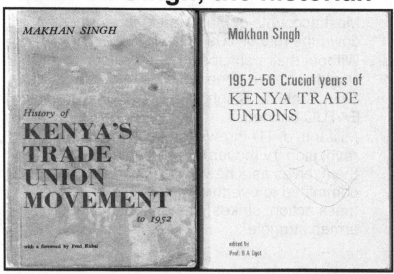

A LIST OF THE PAPERS OF MAKHAN SINGH'S, 1923 - 1973

A. General Correspondence and Papers

B. Subject Files

   1. Trade Union Matters

   2. Detention Proceedings

   3. Bills and Emanual papers during Detention.

   4. Miscellaneous Subject Files

C. Makhan Sing's own Drafts and Writings.

D. Makhan Singh's Notes on his Reading.

   1. Note books kept during Detention.

   2. Notes taken from Archives of various Labour
      Organizations.

   3. Notes on the contents of the East African
      Standard, 1940-50.

   4. Notes taken from material in the Ministry of
      Labour.

   5. Notes on General Reading.

E. Copies of papers presented to the Historical Association
   of Kenya Annual Conferences, 1969-72

F. Press Cuttings

   1. Cuttings on Local Subjects

   2. Cuttings on other areas of Africa

31

A. GENERAL CORRESPONDENCE AND PAPERS

Reference: MAK/A

These files include letters to and from, printed material, press
cuttings, and notes added by Makhan Singh at a later date.

MAK/A/1

   1923, 1926-33. personal papers, many items in
   Punjabi, both print and MS. At fol. 109 is a list of
   Makhan Singh's schools, 1920-31. At fol. 226 is a draft
   of a paper "The Indian Youth in East Africa" c. 1933.
   From fols. 237-39 are pamphlets for the Legislative Council
   bye - election, 1933. 292 leaves (2 files).

MAK/A/2 1934-5. Many items, printed and MS, are in Punjabi. At fol.
   8-10 is a draft speech in East African Union. At fols. 13-27
   are papers about the Kenyan Indian elections of 1934. From
   fols. 56-65 are papers on Hindu customs. fol. 145 passim
   are papers about the formation of the Indian Workmen's Trade
   Union in 1934-5 At fols 162-7 are resolutions of the
   Federation of Indian Chambers of Commerce and Industry in
   East Africa, 1935. At fol. 186-9 is a copy of a petition to
   the Secretary of State for the Colonies concerning the
   removal of the Kikuyu from Tigoni, signed by Luke Wangengu
   and John Mlugeo and including names of Forodiwa, Gizau
   and Staley Kinyanjui, 27 May, 1935. The constitution of the
   Labour Trade Union is at fols. 193-5, with a Punjabi
   translation at fols. 196-203. From fols. 248-58 are papers
   of the East African Indian National Congress, 1935. 264 leaves
   (2 files).

MAK/A/3 1936-September 1937. Many items printed and MS. are in Punjabi.
   From fol. 2 are speeches by A.C.L. De Souza to the Legislative
   Council, 1936. At fol. 17-24 is a political pamphlet "The
   Soul of India," by S.D. Das , 1936, at fol. 28 is "Sheeri's
   Weekly" duplicated in Nairobi, 26 May 1936. At fols. 36-9
   is a copy of a bill to regulate Hindu marriage, 1936. At fol.
   42 is the constitution of the East African Indian National
   Congress, 1936. Throughout are copies of printed material
   for the Labour Trade Union, many in Punjabi, Gujarati and
   Urdu , and press cuttings. The Kenya Worker December 1936
   and January 1937, a newsheet in Punjabi is at fol. 87-102.
   At fol. 117 ff. is material about the Dar-es-Salaam Asian
   Workers strike of 1937 and from fol. 121 ff. material about
   the Nairobi strike of April-June, 1937. From fol. 206 ff.,

The legacy of resistance

The legacy of resistance

The legacy of resistance

Learning from Makhan Singh

. It is as important to understand the reasons that imperialism has sought to marginalise Makhan Singh as it is to understand why information about him has similarly been side-lined by the successive governments in Kenya.

. Such active suppression also affects Kimaathi and the entire Mau Mau movement. It affects progressive activists, thinkers and trade unionists such as Pinto, Kaggia and Kubai. These are not mere accidents of history but active attacks on the forces that support working people.

Learning from Makhan Singh

. Imperialism does not only attack people, leaders, organisations and progressive ideas: it attacks people's history to erase from social memory their very existence so that their example is not followed today.

. It is therefore the first responsibility of those fighting for rights of people to research, understand, practice and popularise working class ideas, leaders, organisations, ideology and actions.

References

Kasrils, Ronnie (2013): How the ANC's Faustian pact sold out South Africa's poorest: In the early 1990s, we in the leadership of the ANC made a serious error. Our people are still paying the price. The Guardian. 24-06-2013.

Kubai, Fred (1969): Foreword to Singh, Makhan (1969): History of Kenya's Trade Union Movement to 1952. Nairobi: East African Publishing House.

Newsinger, John (2006): The Blood Never Dried: A people's history of the British Empire. London: Bookmarks. pp. 186-7.

Ouma, Steve and Makau Mutua (2006): Foreword. Patel, Zarina (2006): Unquiet, The Life and Times of Makhan Singh. Nairobi: Zand Graphics.

Patel, Ambu (Comp., 1963): Struggle for Release Jomo and His Colleagues, Complied by Ambu H Patel, Edited by N. S.Thakur and Vanshi Dhar, New Kenya Publishers, Nairobi, December 1963.

Singh, Makhan (1963): Comrade Makhan Singh's hunger strike for release of Jomo Kenyatta and his colleagues. in: Patel, Ambu H. (comp., 1963): Struggle for Release Jomo Kenyatta and Colleagues. Nairobi: New Kenya Publishers. pp. 138-140.

Singh, Makhan (1969): History of Kenya's Trade Union Movement to 1952. Nairobi: East African Publishing House. p. xi

Throup, David, quoted in Sicherman, Carol (1990): "Ngugi wa Thiong'o: The Making of a Rebel, a sourcebook in Kenyan literature and resistance". London: Hans Zell.

Vita Books Publications

INFORMATION AND
LIBERATION
by Shiraz Durrani
Vita Books, Kenya

KENYA'S WAR OF
INDEPENDENCE
by Shiraz Durrani
Vita Books, Kenya

LIBERATING MINDS,
RESTORING KENYAN
HISTORY
by Nazmi Durrani
Vita Books, Kenya

MAKHAN SINGH, A
REVOLUTIONARY KENYAN
TRADE UNIONIST
by Shiraz Durrani
Vita Books, Kenya

NEVER BE SILENT
by Shiraz Durrani
Vita Books, Kenya

PROGRESSIVE
LIBRARIANSHIP
by Shiraz Durrani

Karimi Nduthu: A Life in
the Struggle
Vita Books and Mau Mau
Research Center, [1998]

Forthcoming

Pio Gama Pinto, the Assassinated Hero of the Anti-Imperialist Struggle in Kenya, 1927 - 1965. Edited by Shiraz Durrani

Pio Gama Pinto was born in Kenya on March 31, 1927. He was assassinated in Nairobi on February 24, 1965. In his short life, he became a symbol of anti-imperialist struggles in Kenya as well as in Goa in India. He was actively involved with Mau Mau during Kenya's war of independence. He was detained by the British colonial authorise from 1954-59. His contribution to the struggle for liberation for working people spanned two continents - Africa and Asia. It covered two phases of imperialism - colonialism in Kenya and Goa and neo-colonialism in Kenya after independence. His enemies saw no way of stopping the intense, lifelong struggle waged by Pinto except through an assassin's bullets. But his contribution, his ideas, and his ideals are remembered and upheld even today by people active in liberation struggles.

Pinto in his own words

Kenya's Uhuru must not be transformed into freedom to exploit, or freedom to be hungry and live in ignorance. Uhuru must be Uhuru for the masses – Uhuru from exploitation, from ignorance, disease and poverty (Pinto 1963).
Pinto was assassinated by the regime on 24 February 1965 and Kenya has yet to replace him - Donald Barnett (1972).

Pio Pinto fell on the battlefield in our common war against neo-colonialism. Along with the immortal Patrice Lumumba ... he has joined the ranks of our martyrs whose blood must be avenged. In such honourable company, his death will recruit new armies of Pintos to continue the fight in which he died [in] the effort to create a united socialist Africa - John K. Tettegah. (1966)

ISBN: 978-1-869886-04-2

PALIAct Ukombozi Library

The Progressive African Library and Information Activists' Group (PALIAct) set up the PALIAct Ukombozi Library, in partnership with Vita Books and the Mau Mau Research Centre in Nairobi in 2017. The Library aims to make available progressive material and to encourage reading, study and research by working people in Kenya.

The need for such a library follows from the fact that progressive literature has been generally ignored by most libraries and learning institutions. Young people with passion to bring about improvement in the country and thirsty for materials that would inspire them in their quest for social justice get disappointed as such materials are hard to come by.

The Ukombozi Library has an initial collection of almost a thousand titles of progressive material, mostly books but also pamphlets, videos and photographs. It incorporates December Twelve Movement's underground library set up by Nazmi Durrani in the 1980s. A majority of these are classics which are either out of print or cannot be found in the local bookshops. Other material has been donated by Mau Mau Research Centre, Vita Books and many progressive individuals active in the information struggle in Kenya.

Membership is open to all who agree with the vision and principles of the

114

library, irrespective of class, ethnicity, religion, gender, region, race or disability. Individuals or institutional membership is available on payment of appropriate fees.

Further information can be obtained from

Progressive African Library and Information Activists (Paliact)

Second Floor, University Way Building Next to Lilian Towers Hotel

P.O Box 746-00200

Nairobi

Email: info.paliact17@gmail.com

Website: http://vitabooks.co.uk/projects-for-change/paliact/

Kenya Resists

Vita Books announces the Launch of a new series for 2018

Vita Books is pleased to announce the launch of a new series of handbooks under the title, *Kenya Resists*. The series covers different aspects of the resistance by people of Kenya to colonialism and imperialism. The handbooks are reproduced from published books, unpublished reports, research and oral or visual testimonies.

The series aims to provide an insight into the history of resistance by people of Kenya. Each number focuses on a specific aspect of resistance before and after independence. The first titles in the series has been taken from Shiraz Durrani's book, *Kenya's War of Independence, Mau Mau and its Legacy of Resistance to Colonialism and Imperialism, 1948-1990* (Nairobi: Vita Books) and from additional sources. The first 3 titles to be published in 2018 in the series are:

> No. 1: **Mau Mau, the Revolutionary Force from Kenya Challenges Colonialism and Imperialism, 1948-63.**

> No. 2. **Trade Unions and Kenya's War of Independence. Includes Reflections on Makhan Singh.**

> No. 3: **People's Resistance to Colonialism and Imperialism in Kenya. Includes presentations on Karimi Nduthu.**

P.O. Box 62501-00200
Nairobi. Kenya
http://vitabooks.co.uk
info.vitabkske@gmail.com

Distributed Worldwide by: African Books Collective
Oxford, OX1 9EN
http://www.africanbookscollective.com/

Printed in the United States
By Bookmasters